The Language of Virgil

FOR CAMELA

PREFACE

As this book goes to press there are some forty beginning Latin textbooks
already in print. It would seem a small blessing indeed to introduce still
another if there were not some compelling reason to believe that this book
has something distinctive to offer. In 1979, a small group of language in-
structors at Northwestern received a development grant from the National Endowment for the Humanities to prepare a set of one-quarter freshman courses
in "The Language of the Masters": Pushkin's Russian, Dante's Italian, Beau-
delaire's French, Homer's Greek, and Virgil's Latin. The object was to teach
freshmen without prior foreign-language background just enough of a certain
language *as used by one of its greatest poets* to understand the particular
virtues of that language, and why the meaning could not be fully appreciated
in any translation. The purpose was not to teach vocabulary or translation
skills, but the character of the language itself as used in its most exact-
ing mode, i.e. in poetry. After three weeks (nine classes) of introduction
to the mechanics, our students were to begin the study of the poetic text itself, unsimplified, knowing just enough to manage the sound and the syntax
on the lines under scrutiny.

The present volume evolved through annual revisions of my course in Virgil's
Latin. Its purpose remains as limited and specific as it was in the beginning. It is a systematic introduction only to such Latin as can be found in
the first 207 lines of *Aeneid* I. The vocabulary and syntax covered are not
intended to represent Latin generally. The effort of a student using this
book should therefore be justified not necessarily as a foundation for future
Latin study but as an end in itself: a taste of unedited Latin, a sample of a
great poem, and an appreciation of what this language can do.   Students
without the time for a more thorough Latin curriculum can now, I hope, have
the opportunity to understand why there is more to language and literature
than their mass-consumption World Lit Surveys can give them.

For the opportunity to undertake this book in the first place, I am grateful
to my colleague John Wright, who designed the joint Language of the Masters
program and persuaded the NEH to make it possible. For constant advice--
some of it exasperated--about the improvement of this book's contents, I am
indebted to the students who sweated their way through any of its early versions. In a sense, it is as much their book now as mine, though I should be
loath to blame them for whatever faults have survived their scrutiny. I owe
a special obligation to my colleagues Jeanne Ravid and Patrick Sinclair, who
took classes of their own through the book and made many useful suggestions.
Finally, I wish to thank the administrators of the National Endowment for
the Humanities and the Research Grants Committee at Northwestern for the fi-
nancial support which enabled the development and publication of this book,
which I dedicate to my daughter as she slugs it out with high school Latin
One.

Evanston, 1983   D.H.G.

INTRODUCTION

The study of Classics has an uncanny appeal. Once force-fed to sullen boys in schools built for the ruling class, it is now discovered by happy accident and enjoyed as a relief from the bleak drudgery of economics and chemistry. Although the snob value of Latin has always been high, its proven educational value is more impressive than ever today, if only for the dramatic improvements which Latin students see in their verbal (and even in their quantitative) aptitude scores. By any measure, Latin has proven its worth not only as a civilizing force but as a discipline which makes its students more fit than others for the mental rigors of professional life.

Reading Latin is a specially satisfying way to stimulate the mind, but few students are lucky enough to acquire a good foundation in their high school years. In spite of a growing demand for good language programs, most high schools have no Latin instruction at all or a weak program, crippled by inadequate funding and overworked teachers. As a result, many excellent students come to college with two or more years of Latin which prove virtually useless in a college-level course. Others come with no classical background but with a natural curiosity about Latin language and literature. Most do not have the time in a crowded schedule for the two years of college Latin which usually precede the reading of Virgil, and these must satisfy their interest with a well-meaning survey of Classical Lit which includes a quick run through some translation of the Aeneid. Like a course in sex and marriage, this will be informative, but no substitute for the real thing.

This book gives you a little bit of the real thing. It cannot replace a regular, systematic introducton to the Latin language, but it contains enough of the language of Virgil to make classical studies less remote and intimidating. It should satisfy some of your curiosity, and it may stimulate you to try more.

Like any profitable enterprise, the task you assume in working through these pages is demanding. This is a work book, not bedside reading, and you must give it your best attention if it is to be worth your while at all. Students who have successfully completed this ten-week course report that it requires, on the average, two hours' preparation for each of the twenty-nine lessons, in addition to class time. They also emphasize that you should pay special attention to the first nine lessons, which contain the foundational material on which the rest of the book depends.

The first nine lessons are Part One, taking you quickly over the fundamentals of Latin that you will need in order to read the beginning of Virgil's Aeneid. There are no vocabulary lists to memorize, but you will learn to recognize the word-endings and the grammatical structure of a language quite unlike any modern language you are likely to have encountered. The mechanical features are what make Virgil's poetry possible.

The rest of the book, Part Two, takes you systematically through the first 207 lines of the Aeneid, divided into twenty short passages. Each passage is translated literally, line for line. On the facing page are listed alphabetically all the words used in that passage, with their English meaning. Above that word list you will find a few notes about difficult points of grammar, necessary background information, and items of necessary interest. After you have assimilated as much of this as you can, you will turn the page and see a clean printing of the same lines, uncluttered with scansion marks and interlinear translation. Facing this version of the text will be a series of questions designed to exercise your understanding of the language and to elicit your insights into Virgil's poetry. No translation will help you with these questions because they have to do with what nobody can translate. The earlier notes, your imagination, and your common humanity will suggest answers, in the writing of which you will be learning--and demonstrating--what poetry is.

Robert Frost said that poetry is what is lost in translation. This course will help you discover why he was right. The objectives of this course are as simple as they are ambitious:

To give you a sense of what Latin is like.

To give you a new way to discover what poetry is.

To give you the experience of Virgil's Aeneid--or a first taste of it. No poetry can be explained. We can explain only what poetry is *about*, but its meaning goes beyond its words. It is an experience, like love (or the measles), and no book or teacher can do more than set you on the road to that experience. If you achieve the ability to understand these lines on their own terms, if you fall in love with them and want more, your sense of poetry and even of life itself will be enriched.

ABOUT THE AENEID

Publius Vergilius Maro wrote the Aeneid a few years before the birth of Christ. He died in 19 B.C. leaving parts of his epic in unpolished form, and ordered in his will that it be destroyed in its entirety. Instead of burning it, his literary executors published it in a corrected edition, and it has been read constantly since then as a masterpiece not just of its period, but of all time. In the Aeneid, Virgil purports to tell the story of the mythical hero who carried the household gods of Troy, after its destruction by the Greeks, to a new land, and how he founded the Roman nation.

The poem sets off the Stoic virtues of Virgil's own time in a favorable light, and shows how the Roman Empire is the final realization of a divine providence whose goal it is to bring order and civilization into the world. But the Aeneid is more than political propaganda and moralistic preaching. It is a personal appeal to grieve at human suffering and to enjoy the spectacle of mighty happenings. His language moves us not only by what it says, but by its sounds and rhythms, as music. Like no other poet, Virgil uses words the way a composer uses the sounds of music, and the effects lend his work a special magnificence. It is intended to be read out loud. It is operatic, romantic, and emotional.

Homer was Virgil's model in the Aeneid. He is constantly borrowing, adapting, or re-orchestrating words, lines, and passages from the Iliad and the Odyssey, always with his own purposes in mind. The Homeric epics were the foundation of a culture that put a premium on individual excellence, pride, quick thinking, and competitive virtues. Virgil focused differently on the purpose of life. For him, the virtues of cooperation, duty, and self-sacrifice were the highest personal goals; the cosmopolis (Rome) presiding over a world order was the highest social goal, and he shaped his epic not only to reflect those values but also to make them exciting. Moreover, Virgil had a basically different idea of poetry. For Homer and the Greeks, poetry should be aloof, Olympian, and impersonal. Virgil strove for a more personal idiom, one which appealed openly to the emotions.

For all of these reasons, the Aeneid must be approached not as a story with a message, but as an actual experience with a meaning. Its chief impact is affective, not simply logical or propositional. It can be compared to a gothic cathedral. You can read piles of art history books telling you about the development of the gothic cathedral. You can pore over floor plans, elevations, and models. You can study color slides of interiors and facades, or contemplate the flying buttress. But none of this can prepare you for what happens to you when you walk into an actual gothic cathedral. Suddenly you feel the presence of God. Never mind if you were an atheist. The presence of whatever it is draws you in beyond all reason or learning. The meaning of a gothic cathedral is what you feel when you are inside it. By the same token, the meaning of the Aeneid is what happens to you when you read it out loud in Latin and understand the words. You are beyond mere translations, professors, grammarians, and footnotes. The purpose of this book is to lead you toward that experience. The rest is up to you.

Allegory of Octavian's victory at Actium
Twenties of the 1st century B.C.
Cameo in the Hermitage collection.

PART ONE

The first nine chapters of this book will serve to introduce you to the nuts and bolts of the language of Virgil. This will be a once-over-lightly approach, not at all a thorough foundation but just enough to help you through the situations we will actually encounter.

It is very important, however, to learn thoroughly the material we will cover during this first three weeks, because unless you understand how and why the language of Virgil fits together, you won't understand the poetry of it. It is exciting to watch a great dancer perform because we know by instinct how the body works and how it is affected by gravity. So also if you understand the joints and muscles of Latin, the magic of Virgil (as well as the music) will come through to you, and you will understand the poem.

Latin differs from English in being an inflected language. The organization of a sentence is signaled not so much by word order as by word ending or inflection. We have some inflection in English: *who* and *whom* are simple inflections of the relative pronoun; *she* and *her* are inflections of the third person singular feminine pronoun. Verbs are also inflected to show person and tense: I *see*, she *sees*, yesterday we *saw*. Inflection in Latin is more complex, as it does most of the work that is done by word order in English. In our language when *Juno sees Aeolus*, it is clear from the word order who is doing what to whom. In Latin that information comes from inflection, so a poet is free to alter the arrangement of words without confusing their meaning, e.g. *Aeolum Iuno videt*. The *-um* at the end of Aeolus' name tells that he is the object which Juno sees.

This is why it is important to recognize word endings and know what they mean. The (to us) jumbled word order in Latin is the most disconcerting thing that faces us when we look at a line of Virgil. But it is well worth the trouble of learning the word-endings and grammar, for an inflected language has a whole range of expressive possibilities not available in a language like ours. Freed from the constraints of a mechanical word order, Virgil can manage more freely the arrangement of sounds and impressions that come over us as we read his poetry. Latin makes possible the famous word-music of the Aeneid.

PRONUNCIATION

The pronunciation of Virgil's Latin is easy because it is consistent. It differs a little from the medieval pronunciation often taught in Catholic and European schools, but it is easy to adjust to even if your ear is already attuned to Church Latin.

<u>Vowels</u> (a, e, i, o, u, and sometimes y) may be long or short:

āter "black": long a as in f<u>a</u>ther   *ac "and": short a as in ide<u>a</u>*

rēx "king": long e as in th<u>ey</u>   *et "and": short e as in g<u>e</u>t*

īra "wrath: long i as in mach<u>i</u>ne   *ille "he": short i as in s<u>i</u>t*
                                                        --or--
                                        Italia: short i as in hol<u>ie</u>st

vōs "you" (pl.) long o as in sm<u>o</u>ke   *aequor "sea": short o as in <u>o</u>bey*

Iūno "Juno": long u as in L<u>u</u>ke   *fluctus "wave": short u as in f<u>u</u>ll*

<u>Diphthongs</u>, being a combination of two vowels, take longer to pronounce, and are therefore long by nature.

ae as in Aeolus sounds like the <u>i</u> in l<u>i</u>ke or the <u>ie</u> in l<u>ie</u>

oe as in moenia "walls" sounds like the <u>oy</u> in b<u>oy</u>

au as in causa "cause" sounds like the <u>ow</u> in c<u>ow</u>

*eu as in Eurus sounds like the <u>e</u> in r<u>e</u>d, plus the <u>oo</u> in sp<u>oo</u>n--this is one
         of the few you will need to practice, because it is foreign to us.*

*Note: there are also a few apparent vowel combinations that are not long
by nature, for example those involving the consonantal <u>i</u>, which is close
to <u>j</u>: Iuno (cf. English Juno), iactatus "thrown" (cf. ejaculate), coniunx
"spouse" (cf. conjugate), iussa "orders" (cf. jussive), Troia (cf. Trojan).
The <u>u</u> after a <u>g</u> as in sanguis "blood" also doesn't count as a vowel, nor
does the <u>u</u> after a <u>q</u> as in qui, quam, or quod. None of these vowel combinations are technically diphthongs.*

<u>Consonants</u> are the same as in English, with these exceptions:

c is ALWAYS hard as in <u>c</u>at, never soft as in city

g is ALWAYS hard as in <u>g</u>et, never soft as in gem

s is ALWAYS voiceless as in <u>s</u>in, never voiced as in rise

t is ALWAYS mute as in <u>T</u>roy, never a fricative as in nation

v is a consonantal <u>u</u> as in <u>w</u>indow, never a fricative as in victor

ch is ALWAYS a <u>k</u> sound, never affricative as in chair

ACCENT: In Latin verse the stress accent is often obscured by the rhythm of the poetic meter, but at least in theory it should always be audible. Like pronunciation, it is easy because it is consistent.

1. Words of two syllables are always stressed on the first syllable:

ÁRMA,   CÁNO,   TRÓIAE,   PRÍMUS,   ÓRIS

2. Words of more than two syllables are always stressed on the penult (the penultimate syllable) when the penult is long:

IACTÁTUS,   IUNÓNIS,   LATÍNUM,   PIETÁTE

3. Polysyllabic words with a short penult are always accented on the antepenult (the third syllable from the end):

ITÁLIAM,   VÓLVERE,   CÓNDERET,   IMPÚLERIT

How do you know whether the penult is long? The Romans knew by hearing the word pronounced, just as we know how to pronounce our much more irregular English. You can use the same method, or look the word up in a Latin dictionary; in this book, long vowels are so marked in each word list.

Mistakes will be made. Classical radio announcers often mispronounce the title of Karl Orff's *Carmina Burana* because they don't know that the *i* of *Carmina* is short--so it comes out "Carmeena Burana." As it happens, that *i* is short, and the accent accordingly falls on the antepenult: *CARmina BurAna*. Next time you hear it mispronounced, call up the station and explain their error. They'll love you for it!

PRACTICE: These words appear in the first few lines of the Aeneid. Read them out loud, following the rules of pronunciation and accent summarized in this lesson.

gentem	pulcherrima	profūgus	Teucrōrum	Mūsa
fātō	iniuria	superum	procellīs	dolēns
gentibus	hīs	caelestibus	Carthāgo	excidiō
animīs	multa	Argīs	Achillī	metuēns
rēgīna	accēnsa	labōrēs	mihi	rēgem
prōgeniem	Latiō	Troiae	ventūrum	moenia
lītora	longē	iūdicium	causās	bellī
terrīs	antīqua	aequora	sanguine	Iūnōnis

Nota Bene: If the words come out sounding a bit Italian, so much the better. Latin is, after all, an Italian language. As in modern Italian, the r sound should have a single roll; double r's should be rolled more fully, and other double letters should be doubly sounded, e.g. procel-līs.

INFLECTION: In English, we signal meaning by inflection of the voice.   In Latin, the words themselves are also inflected.   This is no doubt the most important difference between our language and Virgil's.   As the word implies, inflection is the "bending" of word endings to indicate how words function in a sentence.   In the opening phrase of the Aeneid *Arma virumque cano*, *arma* and *virum* have accusative endings signaling that they are the object of the verb *cano* (*-que*, by the way, is an enclitic form of "and" equivalent to an *et* before the word to which it is attached).   The ending on *cano* tells us that the verb "sing" is first person singular ("I") present indicative active.   You will learn some of the other things it might have been in Lessons 4 and 5.

As a rule, only nouns, pronouns, adjectives and verbs are inflected.   The other parts of speech, namely adverbs, prepositions, conjunctions, and interjections, don't change their form. But although only half the parts of speech are inflected, they constitute most of the words actually used in the Aeneid. Of the 132 words (not counting ten enclitics) which make up the first twenty lines of the poem, only 23 (or 17%) are uninflected.   This means that four times out of five when you look at a word you must understand not only what it means, but what its ending tells you about its use in the sentence, the nature of the action described, and other essential information.

Each inflected word therefore encodes two types of information.   One is *lexical* (telling the meaning of the word), the other *syntactic* (telling how it works in the syntax or structure of the sentence):

A R M A   V I R U M - Q U E   C A N O

lexical meaning +	weapon	man	&	sing
syntactic meaning =	accusative plural	accusative singular		first person singular present indicative active

approximate semantic meaning	I SING OF ARMS AND THE MAN

Now apart from the changed word order in English, one major difference between the two versions is that the English uses seven words to translate what the Latin communicated in three and one half: a ratio of exactly two to one.   This is a little too neat to be true, since only about 4/5 of the words are actually inflected.   But any reasonable statistical test will show how much *more compressed* Virgil's Latin is than the English of his translators.

Here is one simple demonstration. The first twenty lines of the Aeneid contain 137 words, counting the ten enclitics at half a word apiece.   John Dryden's classic 1697 translation uses 229 words to cover the same ground; Robert Fitzgerald's 1983 translation goes on for 246 words, and Allen Mandelbaum's 1971 version uses 238 words.   On the average, therefore, the English translations are using 74% more verbiage than Virgil.

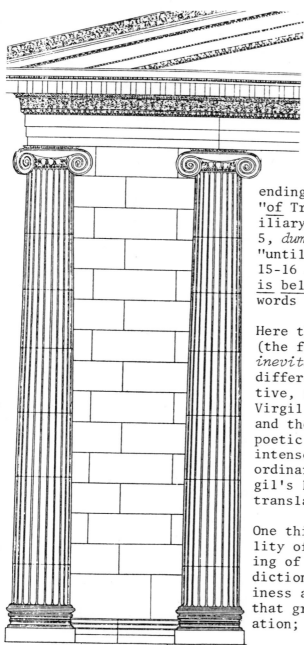

There are other reasons behind the verbal economy of Latin. One is that it has no article, neither the definite article "the" nor the indefinite article "a, an." Another is that much of the work done in English by the prepositions *of*, *by*, *at*, *into*, *in*, *for*, *to*, and the conjunction *than* is usually done in Latin by the case-endings. *Troiae*, for example, is genitive: "of Troy." Latin is also more sparing of auxiliary verbs. The subjunctive clause in line 5, *dum conderet urbem*, comes out in English "until he should build a city." The words in 15-16 *Iuno fertur...coluisse* translate "Juno is believed to have cherished": five English words for two Latin.

Here then is a second aspect of Virgil's Latin (the first was the ordering of words) that is *inevitably lost in translation*. So what's the difference? The difference is chiefly affective, in the emotional content of the Aeneid. Virgil's words are longer, they are weightier, and they carry more meaning. And if we define poetic language as being more compressed, more intense, and more charged with meaning than ordinary language, then it follows that Virgil's Latin is *more poetic* than any literal translation can be.

One thing more needs to be said about the quality of this inflected language. As the bearing of a statesman should be stately, so the diction of epic should have a certain weightiness and grandeur. It must be remembered that grandeur in the Aeneid is not just decoration; it *is* the Aeneid.

The Roman experience as interpreted in the Aeneid, and the Roman language which sets it forth, are inseparable. The medium is the message. When the Queen of England rides down the street in a gilded carriage drawn by eight white horses, it *means* something different than if she went down the same street driving a Toyota.

Roman Bridge at Rimini.

NOUNS

Latin nouns are inflected or declined into six cases.

The nominative indicates the subject of a verb: *Hic currus fuit* "here her
                                                          chariot was."
The genitive designates possession: *saevae Iunonis ob iram* "because of the
                                                          wrath of fierce Juno."
The dative applies to the person or thing indirectly affected by the verb:
                    mihi causas memora "tell the causes to me."
The accusative signals the direct object of a verb: *Arma virumque cano*
                                        "Arms and the man I sing."
The ablative is the case of adverbial relation; it tells how, where, when,
           etc.: *terris iactatus et alto* "tossed on the lands and deep."
The vocative is used in direct address: *Musa, mihi causas memora* "Muse,
                                        tell me the causes."

It is customary to learn the first five of these; the vocative is usually
identical in form to the nominative.

Vocabularies and dictionaries list nouns in the nominative case, followed by
the genitive suffix and the gender: *unda, ae, f* wave; *animus, ī, m* mind.
From this abbreviated information, other forms of the noun can be deduced according to standard rules of formation. The formula also identifies the word
to you as a noun.

There are five types or *declensions* of noun in Latin:

The first declension has a stem in *a*.   The second declension has its stem
example: *terra, ae, f*: earth   in *o*. example: *ventus, ī, m*: wind

	singular	plural			singular	plural
nom.	*terra*	*terrae*		nom.	*ventus*	*ventī*
gen.	*terrae*	*terrārum*		gen.	*ventī*	*ventōrum*
dat.	*terrae*	*terrīs*		dat.	*ventō*	*ventīs*
acc.	*terram*	*terrās*		acc.	*ventum*	*ventōs*
abl.	*terrā*	*terrīs*		abl.	*ventō*	*ventīs*

Second declension neuters follow the same pattern, except that as with all
neuters the accusative is identical to the nominative; note also the *a* ending
                                              in the nominative and
                                              accusative plural.

saxum, ī, n stone   *saxum*   *saxa*
                       saxī   *saxōrum*
                       saxō   *saxīs*
                       saxum   *saxa*
                       saxō   *saxīs*

The third declension includes nouns of all three genders which have a consonant
stem or an -*i* stem.

aequor, oris, n sea   *Iūno, ōnis, f* Juno   *rēx, rēgis, m* king

aequor	*aequora*	*Iūno*	*rēx*	*rēgēs*
aequoris	*aequorum*	*Iūnōnis*	*rēgis*	*rēgum*
aequorī	*aequoribus*	*Iūnōni*	*rēgī*	*rēgibus*
aequor	*aequora*	*Iūnōnem*	*rēgem*	*rēgēs*
aequore	*aequoribus*	*Iūnōne*	*rēge*	*rēgibus*

Third declension -*i* stems have the genitive plural in -*ium*: of ships = *navium*; of nations = *gentium*; of mountains = *montium*; of seas = *marium*, etc.

The fourth declension includes nouns of more than one syllable with stems in -*u*:

fluctus, ūs, m wave

fluctus	*fluctūs*
fluctūs	*fluctuum*
fluctuī	*fluctibus*
fluctum	*fluctūs*
fluctū	*fluctibus*

The fifth declension includes nouns whose stem ends in -*e*; the nominative ends in -*es*:

rēs, reī, f thing

res	*rēs*
reī	*rērum*
reī	*rēbus*
rem	*rēs*
rē	*rēbus*

You will notice that there are strong family resemblances among the case endings from one declension to another, e.g. the final -*m* in the accusative singular, the final -*īs* or -*ibus* in the dative and ablative plurals.

As a reader of Latin, what you must be able to do quickly and automatically is identify case endings: when you see *navibus*, for example, you should be able to conclude without long deliberation that it could be a dative or ablative plural.

ADJECTIVES

As its name implies, an adjective "throws" itself at the noun it describes by agreeing with it in gender, number, and case. Adjectives also follow the nouns generally in their patterns of inflection, although a given adjective doesn't necessarily belong to the same declension as the noun it modifies. They are listed with all their nominative singular forms. Here is a full declension of *altus, a, um*: high, deep.

	masculine	feminine	neuter
singular	*altus*	*alta*	*altum*
	altī	*altae*	*altī*
	altō	*altae*	*altō*
	altum	*altam*	*altum*
	altō	*altā*	*altō*
plural	*altī*	*altae*	*alta*
	altōrum	*altārum*	*altōrum*
	altīs	*altīs*	*altīs*
	altōs	*altās*	*alta*
	altīs	*altīs*	*altīs*

All first/second declension adjectives are listed with the terminations -*us*, -*a*, -*um*, and they are all declined like *altus, a, um*.

Adjectives of the third declension may have one, two, or three terminations.
For us, by far the most frequently seen will be the two-termination adjective
omnis, e: all, every. Note how the vocabulary form differs from *altus, a, um*.

		M & F	N		M & F	N
Singular	nom.	omnis	omne	Plural	omnēs	omnia
	gen.	omnis	omnis		omnium	omnium
	dat.	omnī	omnī		omnibus	omnibus
	acc.	omnem	omne		omnīs	omnia
	abl.	omnī	omnī		omnibus	omnibus

PRONOUNS

A pronoun stands in place of a noun. The most common in the Aeneid is the
relative pronoun *qui, quae, quod*, variously translated *who, which*, or *whom*;
it also serves as an adjective. Most of its case-endings will already be
familiar to you.

		M	F	N		M	F	N
Sing.	nom.	qui	quae	quod	Plur.	quī	quae	quae
	gen.	cuius	cuius	cuius		quōrum	quārum	quōrum
	dat.	cui	cui	cui		quibus	quibus	quibus
	acc.	quem	quam	quod		quōs	quās	quae
	abl.	quō	quā	quō		quibus	quibus	quibus

As in the English "Who was that lady *whom* I saw you with last night?" the
relative pronoun gets its gender and number (in this example feminine singular)
from its antecedent (lady) and its case from its use in its own relative
clause (with whom).

Also very common in the Aeneid is the demonstrative pronoun *ille illa illud*:
he, she, it, or *that*. Like *qui, quae, quod*, it may also be an adjective.

		M	F	N		M	F	N
Sing.	nom.	ille	illa	illud	Plur.	illī	illae	illa
	gen.	illīus	illīus	illīus		illōrum	illārum	illōrum
	dat.	illī	illī	illī		illīs	illīs	illīs
	acc.	illum	illam	illud		illōs	illās	illa
	abl.	illō	illā	illō		illīs	illīs	illīs

From these forms are derived the definite article in the Romance languages,
e.g. Spanish *el* from *ille*, *la* from *illa*, *los* from *illos*, etc.

Hic haec hoc meaning *this* can be used as a pronoun or an adjective, and recurs
with great frequency in the Aeneid. As a pronoun it means *he, she, it*; as an
adjective, it may be translated *this*, as in *haec terra* "this land." The neuter
is often used substantively (as a noun), e.g. <u>*hīs accēnsa*</u> "inflamed by <u>these
things</u>."

		M	F	N		M	F	N
Sing.	nom.	hīc	haec	hōc	Plur.	hī	hae	haec
	gen.	huius	huius	huius		hōrum	hārum	hōrum
	dat.	huic	huic	huic		hīs	hīs	hīs
	acc.	hunc	hanc	hōc		hos	hās	haec
	abl.	hōc	hāc	hōc		hīs	hīs	hīs

PRACTICE

Using the thirteen vocabulary words provided in this lesson, write out the
following forms. Remember that adjectives agree with the nouns they modify
in gender, number, and case.

1. *all seas* in the genitive.
2. *that* king* in the ablative.
3. *high land* in the accusative.
4. *these things* in the accusative.
5. *which wind* in the dative.
6. *all rocks* in the genitive.
7. *deep seas* in the ablative.
8. *Juno's land* in the dative.
9. *those* waves* in the dative.
10. *every thing* in the genitive.
11. *these lands* in the genitive.
12. *all winds* in the accusative.
13. *high rock* in the ablative.
14. *which sea* in the accusative.
15. *this Juno* in the nominative.
16. *all kings* in the ablative.
17. *high waves* in the nominative.
18. *this king* in the genitive.
19. *which rocks* in the dative.
20. *every land* in the accusative.

*Jupiter, disguised as an eagle,
with Ganymede (see pp. 48-49).*

   * use the appropriate form of *ille*.

Translate these phrases into English, using an appropriate English preposition
wherever possible to indicate the case, or an abbreviation of the case in
parenthesis after the English translation.

Examples: *illō ventō* [dat] "to that wind" *or* [abl] "by that wind"
          saxa Iūnōnis [acc] "Juno's rocks"

1. saxa omnia
2. terrārum Iūnōnis
3. cuius fluctūs
4. illīs rēgibus
5. hōc ventō
6. quod aequor
7. altae rēs
8. rēgum omnium
9. cui terrae
10. quōs ventōs

11. Iūnōnem illam
12. quā rē
13. fluctuum omnium
14. hī rēges
15. huic aequorī
16. saxum omne
17. omnēs ventī
18. quārum terrārum
19. illī Iūnōni
20. huius aequoris

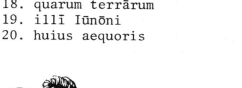

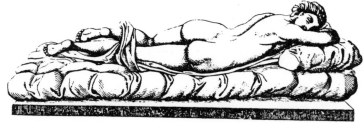

VERBS

Latin tends to rely heavily on its verbs to provide the driving force behind its sentences. Roman writers have a habit of placing much of a sentence's predication (what it says) in the verb.

The Latin verb system is satisfying to learn because it is fairly regular, with relatively few anomalies.

Sum (like the infamous French *être*) is the main anomaly, and a basic verb. Its principal parts are *sum, esse, fui, futurus*. This is its vocabulary form.

Nouns are declined; verbs are conjugated. The conjugation of *sum* includes the following forms.

PRESENT INDICATIVE

1st person singular: *sum* I am	1st person plural: *sumus* we are
2nd " " : *es* you are	2nd " " : *estis* you are
3rd " " : *est* he/she/it is	3rd " " : *sunt* they are

IMPERFECT INDICATIVE

1st person singular: *eram* I was	1st person plural: *erāmus* we were
2nd " " : *eras* you were	2nd " " : *erātis* you were
3rd " " : *erat* he/she/it was	3rd " " : *erant* they were

PERFECT INDICATIVE

1st person singular: *fui* I was	1st person plural: *fuimus* we were
2nd " " : *fuisti* you were	2nd " " : *fuistis* you were
3rd " " : *fuit* he/she/it was	3rd " " : *fuērunt* they were

The forms of *sum* above which appear in the lines of the Aeneid to be read in this course have been underlined.

There are five declensions of nouns, as we have seen. Verbs fall into four *conjugations* whose forms differ slightly but with a strong family resemblance from one conjugation to another. The differences are not terribly important for our immediate purposes, but they are worth noting.

The conjugation of a verb is apparent from its principal parts, which are always listed in dictionaries and vocabularies because they provide the essential information from which all forms of that verb can be derived.

Verbs normally have four principal parts: here is a sample verb.

iactō   is the first person singular, present indicative active: *I throw*
iactāre   is the present active infinitive: *to throw*
iactāvī   is the first person singular, perfect indicative active: *I threw*
iactātus   is the perfect passive participle: *having been thrown; thrown*

The present active infinitive (2nd principal part) indicates the stem from which the present system of tenses is formed; it also shows what conjugation the verb belongs to--the long *ā* of the ending *-āre* marks it as first conjugation.

The perfect indicative active (3rd principal part) supplies the stem from which the past system of tenses is formed.

The perfect passive participle (4th principal part) provides the basis for the participial forms. It is declined like *altus, -a, -um*(p. 7).

TOT·RVINIS·SERVATAM·IVL·CÆR·SIXTI·IIII·PONT·NEPOS·HIC·STATVIT

Principal parts, particularly the second (the present active infinitive), permit you to distinguish between the four conjugations.

Iacto, iactāre, iactāvī, iactātus is a first-conjugation verb, characterized by the -*a* stem. It means *throw, toss*. Because principal parts of first-conjugation verbs seldom vary, its vocabulary form is *iacto (1)*.

iactō	*iactāmus*	The *present indicative active* may be translated "throw, am throwing, do throw." The personal endings attach to the present stem *iact-, iacta-*.
iactās	*iactātis*	
iactat	*iactant*	

iactābam	*iactābāmus*	The imperfect, "was throwing, threw, did throw," designates continuous action in the past be means of the -*ba-* insertion plus personal endings.
iactābas	*iactābātis*	
iactābat	*iactābant*	

iactābō	*iactābimus*	The future "will throw" is signalled in the first and second conjugations with a -*bi-* insertion. This is part of the "present system" of tenses.
iactābis	*iactābitis*	
iactābit	*iactābunt*	

iactāvī	*iactāvimus*	The "perfect system" is derived from the third principal part: "threw, did throw, have thrown." It denotes a single action completed in the past.
iactāvistī	*iactāvistis*	
iactāvit	*iactāvērunt* or -*vēre*	

iactāveram	*iactāverāmus*	The pluperfect "had thrown" denotes action completed prior to some past time: -*eram*, -*eras*, *etc.* is appended to the perfect stem.
iactāverās	*iactāverātis*	
iactāverat	*iactāverant*	

Teneō, tenēre, tenuī, tentus is a second-conjugation verb, characterized by the long *ē* in the second principal part, "to hold."

PRESENT		IMPERFECT		FUTURE		PERFECT
teneō	*tenēmus*	*tenēbam*	*tenēbāmus*	*tenēbō*	*tenēbimus*	*tenuī*
tenēs	*tenētis*	*tenēbas*	*tenēbātis*	*tenēbis*	*tenēbitis*	*tenuistī*
tenet	*tenent*	*tenēbat*	*tenēbant*	*tenēbit*	*tenēbunt*	*tenuit, etc.*

Agō, agere, ēgī, actus "do, drive" is a third-conjugation verb. Note the short *e* in the infinitive and the vowel change in the perfect. The future tense in this and the fourth conjugation has no *-bi-* insertion.

PRESENT		IMPERFECT		FUTURE		PERFECT	PLUPERFECT
agō	agimus	agēbam	agēbāmus	agam	agēmus	ēgī	ēgeram
agis	agitis	agēbas	agēbātis	agēs	agētis	ēgistī	ēgerās
agit	agunt	agēbat	agēbant	aget	agent	ēgit, etc.	ēgerat, etc.

Veniō, venīre, vēnī, ventus "come" is a fourth-conjugation verb by virtue of the long *ī* in the infinitive.

PRESENT		IMPERFECT	FUTURE	PERFECT	PLUPERFECT
veniō	venīmus	veniēbam	veniam	vēnī	vēneram
venīs	venītis	veniēbas	veniēs	vēnistī	vēnerās
venit	veniunt	veniēbat, etc.	veniet, etc.	vēnit, etc.	vēnerat, etc.

Below are the principal parts of verbs which appear often in the lines studied in this course, in order of their frequency. Note that abbreviations tell you only what cannot be supplied from the first principal part.

do, dare, dedī, datus give

sum, esse, fuī, futūrus be, exist

teneō, ēre, uī, tus have, hold, restrain

volvō, ere, ī, volūtus revolve, roll; undergo

agō, ere, ēgī, āctus lead, drive, do

dīcō, dīcere, dixī, dīctus say, speak, tell

possum, posse, potuī be able, can

corripiō, ere, uī, reptus snatch, snatch up

disiciō, ere, iēcī, iectus scatter

faciō, ere, fēcī, factus do, make

ferō, ferre, tulī, lātus bear; report

frangō, ere, frēgī, fractus break, shatter

misceō, ēre, uī, mixtus mix, confuse, stir

mulceō, ēre, lsī, lsus soothe, calm

petō, ere, īvī, ītus seek, head towards

prōspiciō, ere, spexī, spectus look out on, see

tendō, ere, tetendī, tentus stretch; hasten, strive

tollō, ere, sustulī, sublātus raise; stir up; remove

veniō, īre, vēnī, ventus come

videō, ēre, vīdī, vīsus see

vincō, ere, vīcī, victus conquer, surpass

Opposite: the Circus Maximus where Romans went to see chariot-races. Enlarged by Julius Caesar to hold 150,000 spectators and further improved in Virgil's time by Augustus. Subsequent emperors enlarged it to an eventual capacity of nearly 400,000. Like the Colosseum (see p. 24) this was a chief site of mass entertainment. Juvenal complained of the Romans' dependence on "bread and circuses," referring to the grain dole and races in this stadium.

EXERCISES   All of the verb forms below actually occur in the first 207
             lines of the Aeneid.

1. Identify the tense of the verbs listed here by consulting the principal
parts on the opposite page and the paradigms in this lesson; then translate.

   Examples: *posse*--present infinitive, "to be able"
             corripuit--perfect, "he/she/it snatched"

A. *dabant*   B. *mulcet*   C. *tenuērunt*   D. *volvunt*   E. *dederat*

F. *potuit*   G. *facis*   H. *vīcit*   I. *tenuit*   J. *frangere*

K. *prōspicit*   L. *erat*   M. *dās*   N. *dabit*   O. *sumus*

2. Explain the difference between *venit* and *vēnit*.

3. Aeneas tells his men *tendimus in Latium*.   Translate.

4. Write in Latin (omit the pronouns):

A. *he was leading*   F. *it snatched*   K. *it is raising*

B. *she scattered*   G. *to be able*   L. *it rolls (spins, turns)*

C. *it stirs (mixes, confuses)* H. *it was*   M. *she held*

D. *to seek*   I. *they are*   N. *we are*

E. *he sees*   J. *she hastens*   O. *he gave*

MORE ABOUT VERBS

As you have seen, the first principal part of a verb is typically the first person singular, present indicative active. The morphological designation is so long-winded as to call for a word of explanation of why all this fuss.

Most verb forms have the following elements:

PERSON: the first person is *I* or *we*, the second person is *you*, the third person is *he/she/it* or *they*.

NUMBER: singular or plural (Greek has also a dual, for pairs).

TENSE: an indication of when the action is taking place relative to the time of speaking.

MOOD: the way in which the action in perceived--indicative, subjunctive, imperative, infinitive.

VOICE: may be active, e.g. *I see*, or passive, e.g. *I am seen*. Greek has also a middle, *I see for myself*.

THE PASSIVE VOICE

A verb may be transitive or intransitive. In proper English usage, *lay* is a transitive verb, like *see*: it takes a direct object. You see an object, you *lay* an object on the table. An intransitive verb doesn't take an object. *Lie* and *sit* are both intransitive in correct English usage. So are *go* and *fall*. What is the difference between *rise* and *raise*?

Any transitive verb has a passive voice as well as an active voice. In Latin, every active verb form has a corresponding passive form:

vetō	I forbid	*vetor*	I am forbidden
volvit	it turns	*volvitur*	it is turned
frangunt	they break	*franguntur*	they are broken
vīdit	she saw	*visa est*	she was seen
miscēre	to stir up	*miscērī*	to be stirred up
ducere	to lead	*ducī*	to be led

DEPONENT VERBS

You will see these verbs which are passive in *form* but active in *meaning*. They have three principal parts.

First conjugation: *for,* "say" *fārī,* "to say" *fātus* "having said"
                   minor, "jut out, threaten" *minārī,* "to jut out" *minātus* "having jutted out or threatened."

Third conjugation
sequor, sequī, secūtus "follow"
perlabor, -ī, -lapsus "glide through"

Fourth conjugation
coorior, -orīrī, -ortus "arise"
potior, -īrī, -ītus "get possession of"
partior, -īrī, -ītus "divide up"

As a rule, deponents have no active forms and no passive meanings.

MOOD

In the chill hearts of grammarians, mood is understood not as an emotional state but as a modality of action. Most of the verbs you will see in Latin are in the indicative mood. They state a simple fact, as when Aeneas tells his people *tendimus in Latium*--"we are headed for Latium."

--But when a verb does something other than indicate a fact, its modality or *mood* alters.

THE SUBJUNCTIVE MOOD has struck terror into the hearts of schoolboys for generations. Perhaps its subtlety is uncongenial to the adolescent mind. The truth is that it seems only marginally congenial to the Anglo-Saxon mind, as the subjunctive--never highly developed in English--is dying out. Andrew Marvell's seduction ode which begins with the subjunctive *Had we but world enough and time* ... is quaint to the contemporary ear; the avuncular formula *If I were you* is giving way to the crudity of *If I was you*.

The Romance languages (so called because they developed out of Latin dialects) have been less quick to discard the subjunctive. The mother tongue was luxuriant in its uses of this mood; it provides a verbal fine-tuning which comes naturally to a verb-loving language.

The basic effect of the subjunctive is to tone down the force of the matter-of-fact indicative. In our reading of Virgil we will encounter five kinds of subjunctive modulation.

A. INTENTION, EXPECTANCY, OR PURPOSE

In the very first lines of the Aeneid Virgil promises to tell about a hero who suffered much *dum conderet urbem* "until he should found a city." The subjunctive puts a link between the suffering and the founding of Rome which is essential to the poem. Aeneas has a purpose.

In line 20 Juno hears that a people are being preserved *quae verteret arces* "which will overturn the heights" of her favorite city Carthage. The meaning of the subjunctive is lost in translation: "the subjunctive expresses the end or purpose for which the Trojan race was being preserved" (Page).

In 63 Jove puts a king in charge of the winds *qui...sciret* "who would know" when to hold them back and when to let them go. The subjunctive is more explicit: "so that there would be someone who would know...."

In 75 Juno offers Aeolus a nymph *ut tecum...annos exigat et pulchra te faciat prole parentem* "to spend her years with you and make you the parent of lovely offspring."

In 193 Aeneas doesn't stop shooting until he *fundat* (lays low) seven deer and *aequet* (equals) the number of his ships. The purpose of his not stopping is given by the mood of the verb. We see Aeneas in the act of purposeful shooting, not in the completion of his purpose. This refinement of expression is not possible in English.

B. WISH AGAINST HOPE

In 18 Juno hopes that her Carthage may be the seat of empire *si qua fata sinant* "if the fates should somehow permit." The subjunctive here "expresses great doubt and almost despair of the result" (Page).

In 182 Aeneas surveys the sea after the storm *Anthea si quem...videat* "if he might see any[thing of] Antheus," one of his lost captains. He doesn't.

C. CONTRARY - TO- FACT CONDITIONS

In 58f. Aeolus keeps the winds calm; *ni faciat* "if he didn't do so" they *ferant* "would carry" everything away and *verrant* "would sweep" it through the air.

D. EXHORTATION OR COMMAND

After calming the storm, Neptune tells the winds in 140f. that Aeolus should keep to his own territory: *illa se iactet in aula* "let him throw himself around in that court," he says, and *regnet* "let him reign" in the closed prison of the winds.

E. INDIRECT QUESTION

--When a question is not being asked but only referred to; e.g. when Juno asks Aeolus to whip up a storm, the wind-god deferentially replies in 76 "It is yours to explore *quid optes* (what you wish), and mine to take orders."

MORPHOLOGY We will see only the present and imperfect forms of the subjunctive. The present subjunctive simply changes the stem vowel or--in some categories--adds an *a*.

1st conjugation		2nd conjugation		3rd conjugation		3rd conj. *-io* verbs	
indic.	subj.	indic.	subj.	indic.	subj.	indic.	subj.
aequat	*aequet*	*videt*	*videat*	*exigit*	*exigat*	*facit*	*faciat*
iactat	*iactet*			*ferunt*	*ferant*		
optas	*optes*			*fundit*	*fundat*		
regnat	*regnet*			*sinunt*	*sinant*		
				verrunt	*verrant*		

The imperfect active subjunctive adds personal endings to the second principal part, i.e. to the present active infinitive:

   conderet   *inferret*   *verteret*   *sciret*

THE   INFINITIVE   MOOD

The indicative, subjunctive, and imperative moods are finite because their personal endings define their subject. In most instances the infinitive has no subject. Its chief use use is as an indeclinable neuter noun, as the *subject* or the *object* of another verb.

SUBJECT   INFINITIVES: In line 33 *Tantae molis erat Romanam condere gentem,* "(of) so great a task it was to found the Roman race," *condere* is the subject of *erat.* Similar constructions are on lines 96, 135, and 203.

PREDICATE   NOMINATIVES: In line 77 when Aeolus says to Juno *Tuus, o regina, quid optes explōrare labor* "O queen, [it is] your task to explore what you wish," the infinitive is in a predicate nominative relation to *labor.* Similar constructions occur on lines 77 *capessere* and 206 *resurgere.*

OBJECT   INFINITIVES: In line 79 when Aeolus says to Juno *tu das epulis accumbere divum* (you grant [that I] recline at the feasts of the gods), the infinitive is the object of the verb *das.* Similar constructions can be found on line 66 (with *dedit*) and 158 (with *contendunt*).

COMPLEMENTARY   INFINITIVES after *possum* "I am able to --", *scio* "I know how to --", *audeo* "I dare to --", and *paro* "I prepare to --" are actually object infinitives. Examples on lines 38, 39-40, 63, 97, 134, and 179.

INDIRECT   STATEMENT: Verbs of saying, thinking, hearing, and similar mental action govern infinitive constructions in which the subject of the infinitive is accusative. *We hold these truths to be self-evident* is the parallel English construction. This is just another kind of object infinitive.

EXCLAMATORY   QUESTIONS   also use the subject accusative-verb infinitive construction. It is exactly like *What, me worry?* in English. See 37-8, 97-8.

THE   IMPERATIVE   MOOD

The mood of command or request. *Musa, mihi causas memorā* "Muse, tell me the causes." In all conjugations but the first, the imperative singular ends in e: *incute, obrue, age, disice.* In the plural, we will see *maturāte, dicite, revocāte, mittite, durāte,* and *servāte.*

EXERCISES

1. Using the verbs and principal parts given on page 12, write the following in Latin: *they held; to undergo; drive!* (imperative sing.); *she could; they would bear* (subjunctive); *to be stirred.*

2. Write the passive of *fert* and *excutit*; the active of *solvuntur* and *frangitur.* For passive forms, see the middle of p. 14.

3. Identify the person, number, tense, mood, and voice of the following: *disice, videat, dicite, dabit, age, tollere, franguntur, esse, faciat, est, tenuērunt,* and *dederat.* Give the English meaning of each.

PARTICIPLES

As we saw in the last lesson, infinitives are used as a kind of verbal noun; they are usually the subjects or objects of other verbs. Participles provide another form in which verbs can take on additional functions.

In the English sentence *Writing is a demanding art*, the first participle *writing* serves as a verbal noun (subject of *is*), while the second participle *demanding* is a verbal adjective modifying the noun *art*. Another form of verbal adjective is the perfect passive participle: "Juno, *offended* by Aeneas' progress, plans a storm," where *offended* modifies *Juno*.

Given the Latin language's infatuation with verbs, it is not surprising to find an abundance of participles in the Aeneid. The morphology of the participle is simple, easily recognized, and highly predictable.

The *present active participle* invariably ends in *-ns* in the nominative singular; all other forms have *-nt-* plus the third declension case endings (p. 6). The base is the present stem, i.e. the present active infinitive minus *-re*.

The *gerund* and *gerundive* add *-nd-* to the present stem, plus the regular first/ second declension case endings (bottom of p. 7).

The *perfect passive participle* adds those same first/second declension case endings to the fourth principal part.

The *future active participle* substitutes *-rus* for the final *-s* of the perfect passive participle.

	A C T I V E	*P A S S I V E*
P R E S E N T	*servāns, antis* keeping *volāns, antis* flying *tenēns, entis* holding *stridēns, entis* screaming *metuēns, entis* fearing *prospiciēns, entis* seeing	%%%%%%%%%%%%%%%%%%%%%%%%%%% %%%%%%%%%%%%%%%%%%%%%%%%%%% %%%%%%%%%%%%%%%%%%%%%%%%%%% %%%%%%%%%%%%%%%%%%%%%%%%%%% %%%%%%%%%%%%%%%%%%%%%%%%%%% %%%%%%%%%%%%%%%%%%%%%%%%%%%
F U T U R E	*servatūrus, a, um* about to keep *ventūrus, a, um* about to come *datūrus, a, um* about to give *iactatūrus, a, um* about to throw	gerund (verbal noun) and gerundive (verbal adjective) *servandus, a, um* to be kept *tenendus, a, um* to be held *metuendus, a, um* to be feared
P E R F E C T	########################## ########################## ########################## ########################## ########################## ##########################	fourth principal part *servātus, a, um* kept *iactātus, a, um* thrown *datus, a, um* given *commōtus, a, um* disturbed *vectus, a, um* borne

The present active participle is declined like any third-declension adjective on one termination. Here is *servāns, antis*, "keeping."

	SINGULAR			PLURAL	
m & f	n		m & f	n	
servāns	*servāns*		*servāntēs*	*servāntia*	
servāntis	*servāntis*		*servāntium*	*servāntium*	
servāntī	*servāntī*		*servāntibus*	*servāntibus*	
servāntem	*servāns*		*servāntīs (ēs)*	*servāntia*	
servāntī	*servāntī*		*servāntibus*	*servāntibus*	

Note especially the *-i* in the ablative singular and the *-ium* in the genitive plural.

All other participles--the future active, the gerundive, and the perfect passive--are declined like any first/second declension adjective. Here is *datus, a, um* "given."

	SINGULAR			PLURAL	
m	f	n	m	f	n
datus	*data*	*datum*	*datī*	*datae*	*data*
datī	*datae*	*datī*	*datōrum*	*datārum*	*datōrum*
datō	*datae*	*datō*	*datīs*	*datīs*	*datīs*
datum	*datam*	*datum*	*datōs*	*datās*	*data*
datō	*datā*	*datō*	*datīs*	*datīs*	*datīs*

Compare the forms of *altus, a, um* on the bottom of page 7.

Some prominent members of the Julio-Claudian family which ruled the Roman empire for nearly a century. From the left: Claudius, grandson of Augustus' wife Livia and fourth emperor of Rome (41-54 AD); Agrippina, wife of the emperor Tiberius; Livia, Augustus' wife; and her son Tiberius, Augustus' chosen successor as emperor of Rome. See Robert Graves' novel I, Claudius.

THE SYNTAX OF THE PARTICIPLE

Because participles are *both* noun or adjective *and* verb, their function in a sentence is often a double one. Consider the phrase in line 3 describing Aeneas:

> *multum ille et terris iactatus et alto*

> he, much tossed-about on the lands and on the deep,...

Here *iactatus* (from *iacto* (1): toss, buffet) has a nominative masculice singular ending because it modifies and agrees with *ille*; in this respect it is behaving like any adjective.

At the same time, *iactatus* has a verbal aspect; it is modified by the adverb *multum* (much tossed about), and it is further limited by the two ablatives *terris* and *alto*: "on the lands" and "on the deep." Remember that the ablative is the case of adverbial relation, here expressing *where* the action took place.

Here is another example from a few lines later in the poem:

> *id metuens veterisque memor Saturnia belli,...*

> fearing this and mindful of the old war, Saturnia ...

In its character as adjective, *metuens* "fearing" modifies and agrees with *Saturnia*. In its character as verb it takes its own direct object, *id* "this."

In this final example we hear about Pallas Athena's punishment of Ajax:

> *illum exspirantem transfixo pectore flammas / turbine corripuit*

> him breathing out flames from his pierced breast / she snatched up with
>   a whirlwind

As adjective, the participle *exspirantem* agrees with *illum* "him"--Ajax, the direct object of *corripuit*. As participial verb, *exspirantem* takes its own direct object, *flammas* "flames."

THE NEUTER PARTICIPLE AS NOUN

You may already have noticed that two Latin forms given on page 19 are standard English nouns: the neuters *datum* and *data*, "something given" and "things given" can be found in any English dictionary.

iussa (from *iubeo, ere, iussi, iussus*: command) are "commands."
dictum (from *dico, ere, dixi, dictus*: say) is "something said" or a "word."
                                        It is also a standard English noun.

Like neuter participles, neuter adjectives may be used substantively, i.e. as nouns: *multa* "many things," *haec* "these things," *talia* "such things."

Participles of other genders may also have substantive force: *apparent rari nantes in gurgite vasto*="a few [men] appear <u>swimming</u> in the great abyss," or "a few <u>swimming</u> [men] appear...," or "a few <u>swimmers</u> appear." In the phrase *O passi graviora* (from the deponent *patior, pati, passus* "suffer" and the adjective *gravior* "more grevious"), we have two consecutive substantive usages: "O you who have suffered more grevious [things],..."

EXERCISES Translate the following phrases, each of which contains a participle. Be sure the case endings admit the interpretation you propose to put on them. Each phrase is a grammatical construction whose syntax is indicated by the inflection of words. The word meanings are given below. For case endings and their meanings, see pages 6-8 and review this lesson.

1. *dolēns rēgina*
2. *genus invisum*
3. *hīs accensa*
4. *inceptō desistere*
5. *saxa latentia*
6. *indignantes fremunt*
7. *ipsa iaculata ignem*
8. *Ilium in Italiam portans*
9. *populum superbum venturum*
10. *Iuno, aeternum servans sun pectore vulnus,..*
11. *talia flammatō secum dea corde volutans,...*
12. *rēx Aeolus luctantīs ventōs imperio premit*
13. *silent arrectīsque auribus astant*
14. *loca fēta furentibus Austrīs*
15. *conversā cuspide montem impulit*
16. *duplicīs tendens ad sidera palmas*
17. *videt fluctibus oppressos Troas*
18. *motōs praestat componere fluctūs*

accendo, ere, cendi, census: inflame
ad + accus.: to
Aeolus, i, m: Aeolus, the wind king
aeternus, a, um: eternal
arrigo, ere, rexi, rectus: raise
asto, are, stiti: stand near
auris, is, f: ear
Auster, tri, m: the south wind
compono, ere, posui, positus: calm
converto, ere, verti, versus: turn
cor, cordis, n: heart   around
cuspis, idis, f: spear
dea, ae, f: goddess
desisto, ere, stiti, stitus: cease
doleo, ēre, ui, itus: grieve
duplex, icis: double, both
fētus, a, um: pregnant, teeming
flammo (1):* inflame, kindle
fluctus, ūs, m: wave
fremo, ere, ui, itus: murmur, roar
furo, ere, ui: rage, rave
genus, eris, n: race
hic haec hoc: this; he/she/it
iaculor, ari, atus: hurl
ignis, is, m: fire
Ilium, i, n: Ilium, Troy
impello, ere, puli, pulsus: strike
imperium, i, n: rule, dominion
in + accus.: into
incipio, ere, cēpi, ceptus: begin
indignor, ari, atus: be angry, chafe
invideo, ēre, vidi, visus: hate
ipse ipsa ipsum: him/her/itself

Italia, ae, f: Italy
Iuno, onis, f: Juno
Lateo, ere, ui: lie hidden, hide
locum, i, n: place
luctor, ari, atus: struggle
mons, montis, m: mountain
moveo, ēre, movi, motus: move
opprimo, ere, pressi, pressus: crush
palma, ae, f: palm of the hand
pectus, oris, n: breast
populum, i, n: people
porto (1):* carry
praesto, are stiti, stitus: be better
premo, ere, pressi, pressus: keep down
rēgina, ae, f: queen
rēx, rēgis, m: king
saxum, i, n: rock
secum: with him/her/itself
servo (1):* keep, preserve
sidus, eris, n: star
sileo, ēre, ui: become silent
sub + ablative: beneath
superbus, a, um: proud
talis, e: such; neut.=such a thing
tendo, ere, tetendi, tentus: reach
Tros, Trois, m: a Trojan
venio, ire, vēni, ventus: come
ventus, i, m: wind
video, ēre, vīdi, visus: see
voluto (1):* turn over, ponder
vulnus, eris, n: wound

** (1) designates first conjugation
verbs. See page 11.*

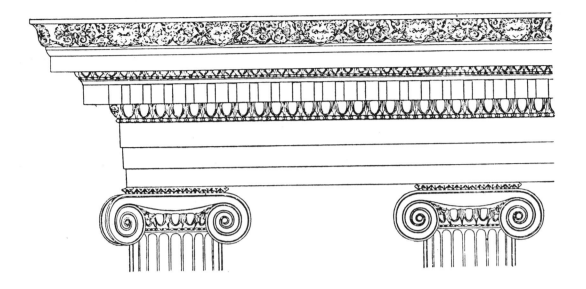

ADVERBS AND PARTICLES

The major components of Latin are the inflected forms of nouns, pronouns, adjectives, and verbs. This lesson presents some minor components that will be encountered in the beginning lines of the Aeneid. Because these do not vary in form, they are easy to learn. They are not inflected.

The largest category is adverbs, which do for verbs what adjectives do for nouns: they are descriptive. Some of them are derived from adjectives: *multum* "much" is the neuter singular accusative of *multus, a, um* "much, many"; *primum* "first" is similarly derived from *primus, a, um*. *Latē* "far and wide, widely" and *longē* "far off, at a distance" are derived from *latus, a, um* "wide" and *longus, a, um* "long" respectively. *Hīc* and *hinc*, "here" and "hence," are offspring of *hic haec hoc* "this," as is *hūc* "hither." *Illīc* "there" has its origin in *ille illa illud* "that."

ante: before

circum: around

citius: more quickly

contra: in reply

desuper: from above

et: even

extemplo: suddenly

forsan: perhaps

hīc: here

hinc: hence, on this side

hūc: hither

iam: now, already

illīc: there

insuper: above

interea: meanwhile

intus: within

lātē: widely

longē: at a distance

magis: more

multum: much

necdum: not yet

nōn: not

ōlim: at some time

post: afterwards

praeterea: hereafter

prīmum: first

quā: in any way, where

quater: four times

quippe: truly, surely

quoque: also

sic: thus, so

super: in addition

ter: three times

tum: then

ubi: where, when

ūnā: together

unde: whence

ut: so that

CONJUNCTIONS

Conjunctions are particles which join elements in a sentence or which join one sentence to another. "And" is a simple copulative conjunction; "but" is one of a type which specifies the relation--in this case adversative--between two parts. These conjunctions appear in the first 207 lines of the Aeneid:

ac, atque: and

ast, at: but

aut: or

cum: when

dum: while, until

enim: for, indeed

et: and

etiam: besides, also

namque: for, indeed

nec, neque: nor, and not

ni: if not, unless

postquam: after, when

priusquam: before

-que: and

quod: because

sed: but

si: if

-ve: or

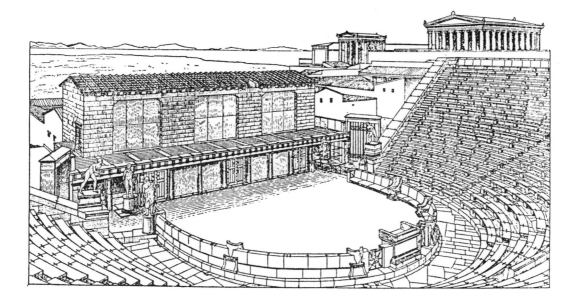

The simple conjunction *et* intensifies its meaning when used in a series: *et terris iactatus et alto* means "thrown about *both* on the lands *and* on the deep."

Aut may also work in a series: *aut Capyn aut celsis in puppibus arma Caici* "*either* Capys *or* the arms of Caicus on his high ships."

The most novel of the conjunctions for the English speaker is the enclitic particle *-que*. In *arma virumque cano* the *-que* works just like an *et* <u>before</u> the word to which it is attached: *arma et virum cano*. The enclitic *-ve* works the same way: *quo numine laeso, quidve dolens* "on account of what offended divinity *or* resenting what..."

Another enclitic particle is the untranslatable *-ne* which introduces a question: *tantaene animis caelestibus irae?* "[is there] such anger in celestial minds?"

PREPOSITIONS

Prepositions are particles which specify the relation of an ablative or accusative noun to its verb. As their name implies, they are normally positioned
before the noun to which they apply.

a, ab: away from, from (abl.)　　　　*in:* in, on, among (abl.)

ad: to, toward, at (acc.)　　　　　　*inter:* between, among (acc.)

ante: before (acc.)　　　　　　　　　*ob:* on account of (acc.)

circum: around (acc.)　　　　　　　　*per:* through (acc.)

contra: opposite, facing (acc.)　　*pro:* before, for, on behalf of (abl.)

cum: with (abl.)　　　　　　　　　　　*sine:* without (abl.)

e, ex: out of, from (abl.)　　　　　*sub:* under, beneath (abl.)

in: into, toward (acc.)

Some words lead double lives: *contra* with the accusative means *opposite*; but
without a noun, as an adverb, it means *in reply*. *Ante*, besides being a preposition taking the accusative, is also a conjunction meaning *previously*.
Circum may be an adverb as well as a preposition. *Cum* as a preposition with
the ablative means *with*; as a conjunction, it means *when*. *Et* usually functions as a simple copulative conjunction, but it may be more emphatic as an
adverb: *timeo Danaos et dona ferentes*, "I fear the Greeks <u>even</u> when they are
bearing gifts."

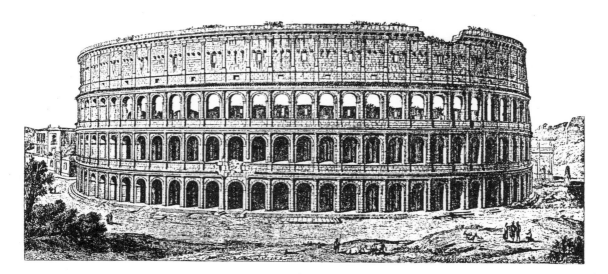

*The Flavian Amphitheater or Colosseum, built in the first century AD
with 87,000 seats, was used for gladiatorial spectacles, bizarre ex-
ecutions, and even water shows featuring sea battles with full-size
ships and heavy casualties. It covered five acres and had a huge
movable awning to protect spectators from sun or rain.*

EXERCISES

Translate, using the vocabulary at the bottom of this page:

1. memorem Iunonis ob iram...

2. unā cum gente...

3. Troiae qui primus ab orīs...

4. ante ora patrum Troiae sub moenibus altīs...

5. Trēs navēs Eurus ab altō in brevia et syrtīs urget.

6. Illā se iactet in aulā.

7. Multōs per annōs errabant acti fatīs.

8. Forsan et haec olim meminisse iuvabit.

9. Hīc currus fuit.

10. Iam tum tenditque fovetque.

11. Hinc atque hinc vastae rupes minantur in caelum.

12. Neque enim ignari sumus ante malorum.

ab, a: from
ago, agere, egi, actus: drive
altus, a, um: high, deep
altum, i, n: the deep [sea]
annus, i, m: year
ante: before
atque: and, as well as
aula, ae, f: court, hall
brevia, ium, n. pl.: shallows,
               shoals
caelum, i, n: sky, heaven
cum: with
currus, ūs, m: chariot
enim: for, indeed, truly
erro (1): stray, wander
Eurus, i, m: the southeast wind
et: and, even
fatum, i, n: fate
forsan: perhaps
foveo, ēre, fovi, fotus: cherish
gens, gentis, f: race, people,
       clan, nation
hic haec hoc: this (see p. 8)
hīc: here
hinc: from this side
iacto (1): show off, flaunt
iam: already, now
ignarus, a, um: ignorant,
          inexperienced
ille illa illud: that
in: in, into

ira, ae, f: wrath
Iuno, onis, f: Juno, Aeneas' enemy
iuvo (1): give pleasure
malus, a, um: evil
memini, isse: remember
memor, oris: mindful, remembering
minor, ari, atus: threaten, tower
moenia, ium, n. pl.: walls
multus, a, um: much, many
navis, is, f:
neque: and not, neither, nor
ob: on account of
olim: some time
os, oris, n: mouth, face
ora, ae, f: shore
pater, tris, m: father, parent
per: through
primus, a, um: first
-que: (enclitic) and
qui quae quod: who, which
rupes, is, f: crag, cliff
se: him/her/itself
sub: beneath
sum, esse, fui, futurus: to be
syrtis, is, f: sandbank, shoal
tendo, ere, tetendi, tentus: strive
trēs, tria: three
Troia, ae, f: Ilium, Aeneas' first home
tum: then, at that time
unus, a, um: one, a single
urgeo, ēre, ursi: drive
vastus, a, um: vast

SYNTAX

Syntax is the ordered arrangement of words in a sentence. In an inflected language such as Latin, this means considerably more than just word order. In Latin, syntax is the relationship of words as signalled by word endings, and the way in which the parts of speech fit together.

You have already seen how a scrambling of words in Latin can take place without seriously dislocating their syntax. This very freedom in the language makes it difficult for us because we are so dependent on word order.

You have also had the opportunity to see that comprehension and translation demand something more than looking up a series of Latin words and making up a story about them. Look again at the diagram on page 4: only about half of the meaning of a Latin utterance is contained in its lexical items, i.e. in the things you look up in a Latin dictionary. The other half, which makes comprehension possible, is syntax.

In the past few days you have begun to learn the essentials of Latin syntax: the basic meaning of the case-endings, the agreement of noun and adjective and of verb and subject, and the uses of uninflected words. Much of what you will learn after this will come to you inductively, by dealing with actual situations without a thorough study of theory. This is the way you learned your mother language; the most important points of grammar are the ones you will see most often. The best way to learn now is to read as much real Latin as possible, with attention to how it works. Once you have gotten some experience with the language, a grammatical rule book like Allen & Greenough's fine old *New Latin Grammar* (still in print after nearly a century) will help you make sense of what you know by experience.

The last few exercises may have caused you considerable vexation and distress. Some of this is inevitable, and it will pass as you get used to the language. Its basic patterns will impose themselves so often that soon enough you will develop the right habits of perception. Nevertheless, a few great truths of Latin syntax bear emphatic repetition at this point in your struggle with the language.

INFLECTED WORDS SIGNAL THEIR AFFINITIES

A. *ADJECTIVES AGREE WITH THE NOUNS THEY MODIFY IN GENDER, NUMBER, AND CASE*

example: SAEVAE MEMOREM IUNONIS OB IRAM (line 4)

Although these linked words belong to different declensions and therefore don't look exactly alike, they do agree with each other. The inflection of *saevae* tells you to look for a noun of corresponding gender, number, and case. In the same way, the adjective *memorem* anticipates *iram*.

In reading this phrase in Latin, you must now do deliberately and consciously what you will later do automatically and unconsciously. Learning any language means more than acquiring a different set of words. Particularly in Latin, it means learning how words point to one another.

B. *VERBS POINT TO SUBJECTS -- SUBJECTS POINT TO VERBS*

example:
> ...*quo numine laeso*
>
> *quidve dolens* ⌐regina⌐ *deum tot volvere casus*
>
> *insignem pietate virum, tot adire labores*
>
> ⌐*impulerit.*⌐ (lines 8-11)

Out of the seeming morass of words above, the nominative *regina* tells you to expect a singular verb: *impulerit* satisfies that expectation.

C. *TRANSITIVE VERBS POINT TO ACCUSATIVE OBJECTS*

In the lines quoted above, *impulerit* points to *insignem pietate virum*, a man distinguished by piety--to do what? Where is the rest of the object?

D. *INFINITIVES ARE GENERALLY SUBJECTS OR OBJECTS OF OTHER VERBS*

More often than not, they are objects, as here we have a pair of complementary infinitives: *tot volvere casus* and *tot adire labores*. The infinitive clauses are also objects of *impulerit*, completing its meaning. When you see an infinitive, you ask "to what finite verb does this relate as subject or object?"

E. *GENITIVES GENERALLY POINT TOWARD -- AND DEPEND ON -- NOUNS*

In paragraph A above, the genitive phrase *saevae...Iunonis* raises the question "fierce Juno's *what*?", a question that is answered when you arrive at *iram*-- "wrath."

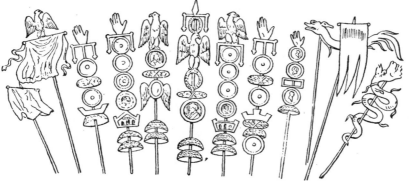

LATIN   SENTENCES   ARE   VERBALLY   ORIENTED

A great chess master once described his game as "fields of force." The same
might be said of Latin syntax, organized as it is around the energy created by
its verbs. If a Latin construction baffles you, the best place to start un-
ravelling it is at its verbs, first finding the main indicative forms and
identifying any subordinate clauses, infinitives, or subjunctives. The main
verb will point to its subject; adverbs or ablative phrases may tell you more
about the action; an accusative will give you the recipient of the action, a
dative will tell you what was indirectly affected. The verb is the mainspring
of a sentence. As you try to solve a syntactic puzzle, look for the action:
who is doing what to whom?

SYNTAX   IS   THE   ASSOCIATION   OF   WORDS

Words which are formally associated--adjectives and nouns, subjects and verbs
--may be widely separated in a sentence and depend upon their endings to point
to each other. In other cases, associated words may be grouped together within a sentence: noun phrases, relative clauses, adverbial phrases, sometimes
marked off for us by editorial punctuation.

The essential thing to remember is that words don't stand alone. They relate
to other words in a sentence. The inflections and the arrangement of words
(word order does mean something in Latin after all) tell you how they relate
to communicate meaning.

EXERCISES

Translate:

1. Urbs antiqua fuit, dives opum studiisque asperrima belli.

2. Celsā sedet Aeolus arce, sceptra tenens.

3. Vastos volvunt ad litora fluctūs.

4. Tantae molis erat Romanam condere gentem.

5. Extemplo Aeneae solvuntur frigore membra.

6. Disiectam Aeneae toto videt aequore classem.

7. Insequitur clamorque virum stridorque rudentum.

8. Aeole, tibi divum pater atque hominum rex mulcere dedit fluctūs.

9. Necdum causae irae saevique dolores exciderant animo.

10. Progeniem sed enim Troiano a sanguine duci audierat. [*See p. 17*]

a, ab: from
ad: to
Aeneas, ae, m: Aeneas, our hero
Aeolus, i, m: Aeolus, god of the winds
  (vocative=*Aeole*)
aequor, oris, n: sea
animus, i, m: soul, mind
antiquus, a, um: old, ancient
arx, arcis, f: height
asperrimus, a, um: most fierce
atque, ac: and
audio, ire, ivi, itus: hear
bellum, i, n: war
clamor, oris, m: racket, noise, clamor
classis, is, f: fleet
causa, ae, f: cause
celsus, a, um: high, lofty
condo, ere, didi, ditus: build, found
disicio, ere, ieci, iectus: scatter,
                    disperse
dives, itis: rich, wealthy
divus, i, m; gen. pl. divum: god
do, dare, dedi, datus: give, grant
dolor, oris, m: grief, anger,
                    passion
duco, ere, duxi, ductus: lead
  (passive infinitive=*duci*)
enim: for, indeed, in truth
excido, ere, i: fall from, perish
extemplo: suddenly
fluctus, ūs, m: wave
frigus, oris, n: cold, chill
gens, gentis, f: race, nation

homo, hominis, m: man [generic]
insequor, i, secutus: follow, pursue
ira, ae, f: wrath, anger
litus, oris, n: shore
membrum, i, n: limb, member, part
moles, is, f: mass, burden, difficulty
mulceo, ēre, lsi, lsus: calm, soothe
necdum: not yet; nor yet
ops, opis, f: resources, wealth
pater, patris, m: father
progenies, ei, f: offspring, race
rēx, rēgis, m: king
Romanus, a, um: Roman
rudens, entis, m: rope
saevus, a, um: fierce
sanguis, inis, m: blood; race
sceptrum, i, n: staff, scepter
sed: but
sedeo, ēre, sedi, sessus: sit
solvo, ere, i, solutus: relax, loosen
strīdor, ōris, m: scream
studium, i, n: zeal, pursuit
sum, esse, fui, futurus: am, be
tantus, a, um: so great
teneo, ēre, ui, tus: hold
tibi: dative, to you
totus, a, um: all, whole, total
Troianus, a, um: Trojan
urbs, urbis, f: city
vastus, a, um: vast
video, ēre, visi, visus: see
vir, i, m: man [gen. pl. *vir(or)um*]
volvo, ere, ui, volutus: roll

WORD

ORDER

At first glance, Latin word order seems perverse and illogical to a native
English speaker, and to anyone else whose language uses word order to desig-
nate syntax. In fact, Latin has a logic of its own in the placement of words
which can be simply stated as two basic principles.

1. *LATIN PUTS FIRST THINGS FIRST*. The most important words come first
in a sentence, with less important elements coming later. It follows the logic of a newspaper writer assembling the paragraphs of a news story. As Allen
& Greenough state the rule, "the word most prominent in the speaker's mind
comes first, and so on in order of importance."

However,

2. *VERBS TEND TO COME LAST*. This is a special tendency of Latin, not by
any means as a rule, but more as an instinct which gives the language its special force.

Most Latin prose can be analyzed according to these two simple rules. When it
comes to poetry, however, other determinants of word order come into play.
For example, Virgil has a metrical rhythm to maintain, and the rules of hexameter verse construction favored word ending in certain parts of the line and
virtually forbade it in others. Moreover, even in prose the Romans (like
their Italian descendents) had a sense of euphony much stronger than our own,
and they sought a sequence of words that *sounded* right. Other aspects of word
music (see Lesson nine) such as alliteration influence the strategy of word
placement in poetry. Line beginnings are places of special emphasis as well
as the beginnings of sentences. There are also some particular patterns which
Virgil and his contemporaries favored as having a certain elegance. This
chapter will introduce some typical patterns of word order in the language of
Virgil.

SYMMETRY

When we look at a Greek or Roman public building, one of the first things that stir us--consciously or unconsciously--is its balance, the symmetry with which each element is set off by a corresponding element on the other side. Poets strove consciously for the same architectonics in the belief that it gave their verbal structures the same grace and dignity.

Here is an example of symmetrical design from the beginning of the Aeneid, the poet's invocation to the Muse:

> *Musa, mihi causas memora, quo numine laeso,*
>
> *quidve dolens regina deum tot volvere casus*
>
> *insignem pietate virum, tot adire labores*
>
> *impulerit.   (lines 8-11)*

"Muse, tell me the causes, on account of what wounded divinity,
or grieving for what did the queen of the gods compel a man
distinguished for piety to turn through so many misfortunes,
to enter so many labors."

Here the Muse comes first because she is foremost in the poet's mind as he prays for inspiration. First he asks her to tell him why Juno was angry; now look at what happens with the words telling what Juno did to Aeneas:

regina deum | *tot volvere casus* | *insignem* | *pietate* | *virum* | *tot adire labores* | *impulerit*.

In this construction the classic pattern of subject first-verb last marks off the pattern. The two infinitive clauses which complete the verb *impulerit* are placed inside these ends, one after the subject and the second before the verb. The distinguished man (the still-unnamed Aeneas) who is the object of the queen's compulsion brackets the *pietas* of the Aeneid's hero as if that virtue were itself a holy icon.

Virgil has accomplished with the peculiar felicity of an inflected language what no English translation can hope to achieve: he symbolizes the theme of his poem in the way he orders his words. PIETAS stands like the central figure in the pediment of a temple.

*Temple of Mars Ultor
in Rome, built soon
after the death of
   Virgil.*

The arrangement of words to frame an element of diction as *pietate* is framed in lines 9-11 is called *bracketing* or *inclusive word order*. The example given there can be schematically represented A, B, C, D, C', B', A'. A simpler example can be seen in the question which completes line 11:

Tantaene animis caelestibus irae?

[Are there] such angers in celestial hearts?

--where the nominatives bracket the ablatives. The simpler A, B, B', A' arrangement is often called *chiasmus*. In normal prose word order *tantae irae* would go together. Any such displacement of ordinary groupings is called hyperbaton, a Greek word meaning a "stepping over," particularly if the displacement is especially violent. The simplest kind of inclusive word order (and the least violent hyperbaton) may be something like *scopuloque infixit acuto* (45), "and she impaled him on a sharp crag," where the sharp crag has itself been impaled on the verb *infixit*. There are many examples in the Aeneid of this type of imitative or mimetic composition.

Another standard arrangement of words is illustrated by the following clause:

crebris micat ignibus aether   *(line 90)*

"The upper air flashes with frequent lightnings."

--where the ablative noun and its adjective are separated by *micat*, and the verb and its subject (linked syntactically if not in normal word order) are separated by *ignibus*. This *interlocking word order* is another way Virgil and his contemporaries had of making the language flow together instead of being a series of discrete word blocks: *crebris micat ignibus aether* is more fluent than *crebris ignibus micat aether*. The ability of his hearers to hold a word in suspension until its partner came along made this kind of composition possible for Virgil. Typically, such constructions involve adjective-noun and subject-verb pairs.

EXERCISES Copy out these excerpts from the beginning of the Aeneid and link the words that go together as illustrated in the diagrams in this chapter. Then translate.

Example: *Cavum conversā cuspide montem impulit.*

He struck the hollow mountain with his turned-about spear.

1. ...et pulchrā faciat te prole parentem.
2. Sēnsit Neptunus imīs stagna refusa vadīs.
3. Horrentī atrum nemus imminet umbrā.
4. Summā placidum caput extulit undā.
5. Disiectam Aeneae totō videt aequore classem.
6. Egressi optatā potiuntur Troes harenā.
7. Hīc fessas non vincula navīs ulla tenent.
8. Tantane vos generis tenuit fiducia vestri?
9. Rotīs summas levibus perlabitur undas.

Aenēas, ae, m: Aeneas
aequor, oris, n: the sea
āter, tra, trum: black
caput, itis, n: head
classis, is, f: fleet
disicio, ere, iēci, iectus: scatter
effero, erre, extuli, ēlātus: lift out
ēgredior, i, gressus: step out
et: and
facio, ere fēci, factus: make
fessus, a, um: weary
fiducia, ae, f: confidence
genus, eris, n: race, family
harēna, ae, f: sand, beach
hīc: here
horreo, ēre, ui: quiver
immineo, ēre: overhang
īmus, a, um: deepest
levis, e: light
navis, is, f: ship
nemus, oris, n: grove
Neptūnus, i, m: god of the sea
-ne: interrogative enclitic
nōn: not
opto (1): wish, long for

parens, entis, m: father, parent
perlābor, i, lapsus: glide over
placidus, a, um: serene
potior, iri, itus: (with abl.) win
prōles, is, f: offspring
pulcher, chra, chrum: pretty
refundo, ere, fudi, fusus: pour back
rota, ae, f: wheel
sentio, ire, sensi, sensus: sense
stagnum, i, n: still water
summus, a, um: top, the top of
tantus, a, um: so great
tē: abl. or accus., you (singular)
teneo, ēre, tenui, tentus: possess
totus, a, um: whole
Trōs, Trōis, m: a Trojan
ullus, a, um: any
umbra, ae, f: shade
unda, ae, f: wave
vadum, i, n: depth
vester, tra, trum: your (pl.)
video, ēre, vīdi, vīsus: see
vinculum, i, n: chain
vōs: you (nom. or acc. plural)

WORD   MUSIC

Some of the spell which Virgil cast over his first listerers--and over readers for some 2000 years since--comes from the sheer *sound* of his poetry. Like the best of Shakespeare, Virgil's language fills the mouth and the ear in a way which gives great pleasure. It is sonorous: full, deep, and rich. It has a powerful, impressive sound, perfectly suited to its grand subject. John Dryden's seventeenth century translation was perhaps the most successful in bringing Virgil's sound over into English, but his version seems archaic to our ears. No twentieth century translation comes near to What Virgil composed, perhaps because grandeur is not a twentieth century virtue. Beethoven's Ninth Symphony doesn't sound right on an electric guitar.

Few poets of any age or language have succeeded as Virgil did in exploiting the musical properties of their verbal medium. When Virgil started his epic *Arma virumque cano*, "Arms and the man I sing," he was writing in the bardic tradition according to which poetry was sung, or at least recited in a quasi-musical chant accompanied by the lyre. The term "lyric poetry" is another memory of the poet as singer, and it is a good bet that the only poetry most people can recite today on a moment's notice is the lyrics of a popular song--and they will probably remember the lyrics better if they hear the music. Virgil took the association of poetry and music more seriously than most practitioners of his craft. The word music of the Aeneid is therefore an important (and untranslatable) part of the poem.

Three important elements of music are rhythm, tempo, and tone. Each of these has its part to play the the Aeneid.

RHYTHM   has its own built-in associations. Anybody can tell the difference between a march and a waltz, and will respond instinctively in a different way to each.   One makes you feel like a parade, the other like romantic dancing. Virgil's rhythm--his meter-- elicited an epic mood because it was the meter of Homer and his imitators for centuries.   It had built in associations of great battles, mighty heroes, and important events. Its movement is swift but at the same time stately, and it has enough flexibility to avoid monotony. These were fortunate advantages, because Virgil's choice of meter was dictated by convention.

<u>Dactylic hexameter</u> gets its name from its basic metrical unit, the dactyl, whose rhythm is the same as that of its name in Greek: δάκτυλος or *dactylos,* two longs and a short marked ⎯⏑⏑. There are six dactyls in each line, hence the name *hexameter.* Its flexibility is built-in by the option of *substitution.* In any of the first four feet, a *spondee* (⎯⎯) may be substituted for a dactyl. The resultant scheme looks like this:

$$\acute{\overline{}}\,\overline{\smile\smile}\,\Big|\;\acute{\overline{}}\,\overline{\smile\smile}\,\Big|\acute{\overline{}}\,\overline{\smile\smile}\Big|\acute{\overline{}}\,\overline{\smile\smile}\Big|\acute{\overline{}}\,\smile\smile\Big|\acute{\overline{}}\,\times$$

The fifth foot is rarely a spondee, and the sixth foot is always disyllabic without regard to the quantity of its last syllable. The accent mark over the first syllable of each foot is the *beat.* Unlike most popular music, Virgil's hexameter has a weak beat, more felt than heard.

STRESS-ACCENT vs. PITCH-ACCENT

The difference between a long and a short syllable in Latin hexameter verse is purely quantitative with respect to its duration in time. It is exactly like the difference between the long half note and the short quarter note. You don't sing half notes louder than quarter notes; you simply dwell longer on them. Quantitative verse employs a pitch-accent as opposed to the stress-accent of qualitative verse. Note the regular stress-accents in this dactylic line of Longfellow:

thís is thĕ|*fórĕst prĭméval, thĕ*|*múrmŭrĭng*|*píne ănd thĕ*|*hémlŏck*

Here, as generally in English verse, the stress-accents correspond to the beat of the line. No beat is heard in the Latin hexameter; it is a "sung" meter.

This difference is harder for some beginners to master than Latin syntax, but it is nearly as important, because the sound of Virgil is nearly as important as his sense. Remember as you read his lines that they follow a *pitch* accent; so pitch your voice a little lower for the short ones. Remember too that the rhythm is quantitative, so spend longer pronouncing the long syllables than you do on the short ones:

Ārmă vĭrūmquĕ cănō, Trōiae qui prīmŭs ăb ōrīs

Ītăliăm fātō prŏfŭgŭs Lāvīnăquĕ vēnĭt

lītŏră; mūltum ĭllĕ ĕt tērrīs iāctātŭs ĕt āltō

vī sŭpĕrŭm, saevae mĕmŏrĕm Iūnōnĭs ŏb īram ...

Prose accent, i.e. the rules of accentuation that you learned in the first chapter, tends to get lost as we read these lines, although ideally—being accent and not tone—it should also be audible.

Notice that in the third line there are two *elisions* where the last syllable
of one word and the first syllable of the next are pronounced as a single
sound. The rule is simple: final vowels and final *m*'s are elided with initial
vowels. Initial *h*'s are so weak that they are ignored in scansion: *animam
hanc* is therefore elided into three syllables. No one is certain just what
elisions sounded like; final *m*'s may have just dropped out, though some say
both should be lightly sounded, as in modern opera. Some lattitude is therefore accepted in the management of elisions, though there is no doubt about
where they are observed.

Scansion itself is easily learned both intellectually and on the ear; with a
little practice you will be able to scan at sight without even marking off the
long and short syllables.

How does one know when a syllable is long and when it is short? The native
speaker's answer is that you know from the way a word sounds, but since there
are no more native speakers around, that answer will no longer do. A syllable
gets its length from the quantity of its vowel. A vowel may be long *by nature*
--like the *ē* in *rēx* or the *ā* in the ablative singular ending of the first declension. You learn those quantities when you learn those words and those
endings. A vowel may also be long *by position*; this does not alter the pronunciation of that vowel itself, but it does make the syllable long; a vowel
"makes position" when it preceded two consonants or a double consonant such as
x (*ks*). A diphthong is long by nature, and makes the syllable in which it
falls long also. Anything which makes the syllable longer to pronounce makes
it long.

The best way to learn scansion is to memorize as little as ten or a dozen
lines of verse. The rhythm must be learned *instinctively* and by feel, not
just as an intellectual concept.

TEMPO is the speed at which music is played. Although the Virgilian
metronome keeps a more or less constant pace, the *apparent* speed of his verse
may be fast or slow as the occasion demands. Notice, for example, the dramatic change of pace in this storm scene:

> Frānguntūr rēmī, tūm prōrā avērtĭt ĕt undīs
>
> dăt lătŭs; īnsĕquĭtūr cŭmŭlō praerŭptŭs ăquae mŏns.

The substitution of spondees for dactyls wherever possible in the first line
and their avoidance until the fourth foot in the second accounts for the difference. Such calculated manipulations of speed, sometimes within a single
line, are an untranslatable part of Virgil's musical art.

TONE is another variable, not in the sense of pitch or melody but in the
sense of tonality or tone color. At the beginning of this chapter we described Virgil's style as sonorous. The first three words of the poem are
just right not only because they say the right things but also because *arma
virumque cano* has a fine, drum-rolling, deep impressiveness about it, thanks
to the repetition of *rm* sounds in *arma virum* and the preference of open or
long vowel sounds (*a*'s and the long *ō*) to short, closed vowels. The verb *volvo*
appears often in the lines we will read not just because things are rolling
around a lot but because of that verb's peculiar sonority, as heard for example in line 86: *vastos volvunt ad litora fluctus.*

This brings us to a final aspect of Virgilian word music to which it is difficult to assign a musical term. Because words themselves cannot take on a me-
lodic line, Virgil is heavily dependent on the percussion section of his or-
chestra. Deep answers deep in the music of Virgil when sounds repeat themselves in *alliteration*. Listen to the rolling thunder of the storm in

>   *Interea magno misceri murmure pontum*
>
>   *emissamque hiemem ...*

--or hear Aeolus knocking on his mountain in c͟avum c͟onversa c͟uspide montem.
In the previous lesson we saw an example of the mimetic ordering of words; no
less effective is Virgil's orchestration of word sounds to give force to his
descriptions. The effects are always impressive, and this is why it is so important to read Virgil OUT LOUD !

EXERCISES

> *O socii (neque enim ignari sumus ante malorum),*
> *o passi graviora, dabit deus his quoque finem.*
> *Vos et Scyllaeam rabiem penitusque sonantis*
> *accestis scopulos, vos et Cyclopia saxa*
> *experti: revocate animos maestumque timorem*
> *mittite; forsan et haec olim meminisse iuvabit.*
> *Per varios casus, per tot discrimina rerum*
> *tendimus in Latium, sedes ubi fata quietas*
> *ostendunt; illic fas regna resurgere Troiae.*
> *Durate, et vosmet rebus servate secundis.*

These are the last verses of our selection from the beginning of the Aeneid.
Copy them out; mark in the scansion, using as a model the scansion of lines
1-4 on page 35 (be sure to mark elisions). Remember that the last five syllables of each line do not vary. Read the lines out loud until you can render
this speech of Aeneas to his people in a convincing manner. These would be
excellent lines to memorize.

PART TWO

INTRODUCTION

You are now ready to begin the Aeneid itself. You have already seen some of
it in disconnected pieces, and you have been introduced to the most common
vocabulary and constructions. In the pages which follow, you will study the
first 207 lines of the poem in sections of about ten lines each. In each of
these sections you are provided with an interlinear translation of the text,
with scansion. Like all crutches, the translations are stiff and wooden, and
their only purpose is to help you over any difficulty you may have in seeing
how Virgil's Latin is fitting together. The scansion marks are to help you
read the Latin out loud without wasting any time on the mechanics of scansion.
Facing each page is an alphabetical list of the vocabulary form of every word
that occurs in that passage, so you won't have to waste time thumbing through
a Latin dictionary. Above the vocabulary are a few notes on the text.

Study each passage carefully until you understand the syntax completely and
have absorbed the meaning well enough to read the Latin *without translating*.
This is not a course in translating Latin; it is a course in the language of
Virgil, and as long as you are merely translating you are not understanding
the language. Read the passage out loud, following the scansion marks, until
you are reading metrically at a reasonably fast pace. At first, this whole
business will take you a long time, but don't get discouraged; what you are
doing is difficult but very worthwhile. It will come faster later on.

Once you have mastered the passage, turn the page. There you will find a
clean copy of the same text and a few questions about it. Ideally, you should
be able to answer them without looking back at the "crutch" pages.

At first the questions will be mainly mechanical, but we will concentrate in-
creasingly on literary matters as your mastery of the language develops.

MAP 14
ANCIENT ITALY
Scale of Miles
0   50   100

Arma virumque: Virgil announces his dual Homeric theme by alluding to Iliadic "arms" and the study of a "Man," the first word of the Odyssey. Troiae: Virgil follows the tradition that Rome was founded by refugees from Troy.

3 iactatus: the theme of the suffering hero. Cf. profugus (2), passus (5), passus (9), and labores (10).

5-6 for dum and the subjunctives conderet and inferret, see page 15.

8 Musa: the traditional epic prayer to the Muse for inspiration.

9 regina. Juno is the hostile deity who persecutes the hero in this epic, as Homer's Poseidon persecuted Odysseus. deum: shortened from deorum; cf superum.

10 pietate: a thematic word for Aeneas. In Latin, this is more than religious zeal; it includes duty to gods, ancestors, family, nation, posterity--for Virgil, even civilization itself. It is sometimes translated "goodness" or "duty," but there is no corresponding English word. labores: like the "labors" of Hercules, a favorite hero of the time; but they also imply pain.

ā, ab: from
adeo, ire, ivi, itus: enter, approach
Albānus, a, um: Alban; from Alba Longa
altus, a, um: high
arma, orum, n: arms, equipment, tools
atque: and
bellum, i, n: war
cano, ere cecini, cantus: sing
cāsus, ūs, m: chance, misfortune
causa, ae, f: cause
condo, ere, didi, ditus: found
deus, i, m: god (gen. pl. = deum)
doleo, ēre, ui, itus: grieve
dum + subjunctive: until
fātum, i, n: fate
genus, eris, n: race, family
iacto (1): throw around, toss, buffet
ille, illa, illud: that; he, she, it
impello, ere, puli, pulsus: compel
infero, ferre, tuli, lātus: bring into
insignis, e: distinguished, marked
īra, ae, f: anger, ire, wrath
Italia, ae, f: Italy
Iūnō, ōnis, f: Juno, wife of Jove
labor, ōris, m: hardship, task
laedo, ere, si, sus: wound, offend
Latīnus, a, um: Latin; from Latium
Latium, i, n: the part of Italy around Rome
Lavinus, a, um: Lavinian; Italian
lītus, oris, n: shore
memor, oris: mindful, remembering
memoro (1): recall, recount
mihi: dative, to me
moenia, ium, n: walls
multum: much
Mūsa, ae, f: the Muse

nūmen, inis, n: divinity, divine power
ob: on account of
ōra, ae, f: shore, coast, region
pater, tris, m: father
patior, pati, passus: suffer, endure
pietas, atis, f: loyalty, duty
primus, a, um: first
profugus, i, m: fugitive, refugee
qui, quae, quod: who, which
quid: interrog. pron.= what?
quoque: also
rēgina, ae, f: queen
Rōma, ae, f: Rome
saevus, a, um: cruel, savage, fierce
superi, erum, m: those above, the gods
tot: so many (indeclinable)
terra, ae, f: land
Troia, ae, f: Troy, Ilium
unde: whence, from which
urbs, urbis, f: city
-ve: (enclitic) or
venio, ire, vēni, ventus: come, go
vir, i, m: man
vīs, vis, f: force, strength
volvo, ere, ui, volutus: roll through

ARRIVAL OF AENEAS IN LATIUM.

I sing of arms and the man who first from the shores of Troy
Armă vĭrūmquĕ cănō, Trōiaē quī prīmŭs ăb ōrĭs

came to Italy and the Lavinian shores,   by fate an exile--
Itălĭam fātō prŏfŭgūs Lāvīnăquĕ vēnĭt

he much tossed about both on the lands and on the deep
3   lītŏră--mūltum ĭllĕ ĕt tērrīs īactātŭs ĕt āltō

by the force of the gods, because of the remembering wrath of
vī sŭpĕrūm, saēvaē mĕmŏrēm Iūnōnĭs ŏb Īrăm,   *savage Juno,*

and having suffered many things also in war, until he should
mūltă quŏquĕ ĕt bēllō pāssŭs, dūm cōndĕrĕt ūrbĕm   *build a city*

and bring (his) gods into Latium--whence the Latin race
6   īnfērrētquĕ dĕōs Lătĭō--gĕnŭs ūndĕ Lătīnŭm

and the Alban fathers and the walls of high Rome.
Ālbānīquĕ pătrēs ātquĕ āltaē moēnĭă Rōmaē.

Muse, tell me the causes, for what divinity wounded
Mūsă, mĭhī caūsās mĕmŏră, quō nūmĭnĕ laēsŏ

or grieving for what did the queen of the gods compel
9   quĭdvĕ dŏlēns rēgīnă dĕūm tōt vōlvĕrĕ cāsŭs

a man distinguished for pietas to circle through so many mis-
īnsīgnēm pĭĕtătĕ vĭrŭm, tŏt ădīrĕ lăbōrĕs   *fortunes,*

to enter so many labors.
Īmpŭlĕrĭt.

Augustus' wife Livia as a personification of pietas

EXERCISES

1. Make a list of all nominative forms in this passage, another list of the genitive forms, and so on with the dative, accusative, ablative, and vocative cases.

2. Explain the syntax of every ablative form by naming the type of construction and the verbal dependence. With adjectives, it will probably be because they agree with some ablative noun; if so, which one? You will find ablatives of attendant circumstance, cause, means (instrumental abl.), place where, and separation.

EXAMPLE: pietate (10) ablative of cause, depending on insignem (it tells why Aeneas was distinguished).

The Gemma Augustea, showing Augustus seated next to the goddess Roma, being crowned by Orbis Romanus. Roman soldiers in the lower zone bring in prisoners and raise a trophy (like the Marines in the Iwo Jima photo).

Arma virumque cano, Troiae qui primus ab oris

Italiam fato profugus Lavinaque venit

3 litora--multum ille et terris iactatus et alto

vi superum, saevae memorem Iunonis ob iram,

multa quoque et bello passus, dum conderet urbem

6 inferretque deos Latio--genus unde Latinum

Albanique patres atque altae moenia Romae.

Musa, mihi causas memora, quo numine laeso

9 quidve dolens regina deum tot volvere casus

insignem pietate virum, tot adire labores

impulerit.

*11 irae: one of many "poetic plurals"; cf. irarum and dolores (25) furias (41)
claustra (56), iras (57), sceptra (78), irae (130), etc. Virgil's question in
line 11 underlines a religious problem which troubled the people of his time:
why are the traditional Olympian gods so ungodlike in their passions and ven-
dettas? How can they be just gods and fickle personalities at the same time?*

*12 antiqua "implies not only age, but the honor due to age." (Austin) Tenuēre
is a shortened form of tenuērunt; see p. 11.*

*16 posthabitā Samō: ablative absolute, an idiom awkward in English. Samos is
an island close to modern Turkey whose earliest inhabitants worshipped a goddess later identified with Hera or Juno. The ruins of her temple can still be
seen there. Coluisse: infinitive in the perfect tense; syntax: see p. 17.*

*17 hoc...esse: indirect statement construction, object of tenditque fovetque.
The subject of the infinitive is regularly accusative.*

18 sinant: for the subjunctive, see p. 16, B.

19 duci is a present passive infinitive; see p. 14 for the passive voice.

*20 Tyrias...quae verteret arces: imperfect subjunctive denoting futurity; see
p. 15, A. Virgil alludes to the Punic Wars between Rome and Carthage ("Tyrian" because Carthage was originally a colony of Phoenician Tyre), which ended
with the sack of Carthage in 146 B.C.*

a, ab: from
animus, i, m: soul, spirit, mind
antīquus, a, um: ancient
arx, arcis, f: citadel, fort, height
arma, orum, n: arms, gear, equipment
asperrimus, a, um: most harsh
audio, ire, ivi, itus: hear
bellum, i, n: war
caelestis, e: heavenly
Carthago, inis, f: Carthage
colo, ere, ui, cultus: cherish
colōnus, i, m: colonist, settler
contrā: opposite, facing
currus, ūs, m: chariot
dea, ae, f: goddess
dīves, divitis: rich
duco, ere, duxi, ductus: lead, bring
enim: for, indeed, in truth
esse: (see *sum*)
fatum, i, n: fate
fero, ferre, tuli, lātus: bear; say
foveo, ēre, fovi, fotus: cherish
fuit: (see *sum*)
gens, gentis, f: clan, race, nation
hic, haec, hoc: this
hīc: here
iam: now, already
ille, illa, illud: that; he, she, it
īra, ae, f: ire, anger, wrath
Italia, ae, f: Italy

Iūnō, ōnis, f: Juno, Jupiter's wife
longē (adv): far, at a distance
magis: more, rather
ōlim: at one time, once
omnis, e: all, every
ops, opis, f: resources, wealth
ostium, i, n: mouth, entrance
posthabeo, ēre, ui, itus: esteem less
prōgeniēs, ei, f: progeny, offspring
qui quae quod: who, which
quā: in any way; where
rēgnum, i, n: reign, dominion
Samos, i, f: the island of Samos
sanguis, inis, m: blood
sed: but
si: if
sino, ere, sivi, situs: allow
studium, i, n: zeal, pursuit
sum, esse, fui, futurus: be, exist
tantus, a, um: so great
tendo, ere, tetendi, tentus: strive
teneo, ēre, ui, tus: have, hold
terra, ae, f: land, earth
Tiberīnus, a, um: of the Tiber river
Troiānus, a, um: Trojan
tum: then, at that time
Tyrius, a, um: Tyrian, Carthaginian
unus, a, um: one; only, alone
urbs, urbis, f: city
verto, ere, i, rsus: turn, overturn

Is there such anger in celestial hearts?
Tāntaēnĕ‿ănĭmīs cāelēstĭbŭs īrāe?

12 *There was an ancient city (Tyrian colonists inhabited it),*
Ūrbs āntīquă fŭit (Tȳrĭī tĕnŭērĕ cŏlōnī)

Carthage, opposite Italy and Tiber's mouths at a distance,
Cārthāgŏ,‿Ĭtălĭām cōntrā Tĭbĕrīnăquĕ lōngē

rich in wealth and most harsh in the pursuits of war;
ōstĭă, dīvĕs ŏpūm stŭdĭīsquĕ‿āspērrĭmă bēllī;

15 *which Juno is said to have cherished alone more than all lands,*
quām Iūnō fērtūr tērrīs măgĭs ōmnĭbŭs ūnăm

Samos having been esteemed less: here were her arms,
pōsthăbĭtā cŏlŭīssĕ Sămō: hīc īllĭŭs ārmă,

Fig. 1

here her chariot; that this would be a ruler to the nations,
hīc cūrrūs fŭit; hōc rēgnūm dĕă gēntĭbŭs ēssĕ,

18 *if somehow the fates should permit, already at that time she strives for*
sī quā fātă sĭnānt, iām tūm tēndĭtquĕ fŏvētquĕ.   *and cherishes.*

But yet she had heard that a race was being brought from Trojan blood
Prōgĕnĭēm sĕd ĕnīm Trōĭănŏ‿ā sānguĭnĕ dūcī

20 *which one day would overturn the Tyrian citadels;*
āudĭĕrāt Tȳrĭās ōlĭm quāe vērtĕrĕt ārcĕs;

Fig. 2

Fig. 1: *Samian coin showing Hera in her temple.*
Fig. 2: *Ancient coin--Hera with arms and chariot.*

EXERCISES

1. Identify the person, number, tense, mood and voice of the thirteen verb
   forms in this passage. N.B.: The interrogative enclitic -*ne* (11) is not
   a verb. The verb in this first line is understood. Its omission is called
   ellipsis.

2. Explain the reasons for the gender, number and case of *quam* (15) and *quae*
   (20). For the rule of syntax, see the middle of page 8.

3. Explain the syntax of the infinitive mood in lines 16 (*coluisse*) and 19
   (*duci*). The rules are on page 17.

4. You may already have noticed how casually Virgil shifts from the perfect to
   the historical present. Give one or two examples from this passage.

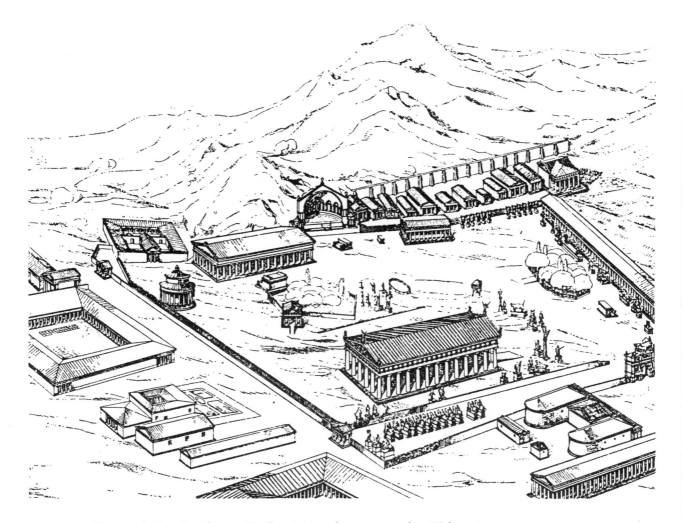

The original site of the Olympic games in Elis, Greece,
as it appeared in Roman times.

                    Tantaene animis caelestibus irae?

12   Urbs antiqua fuit (Tyrii tenuere coloni)

          Carthago, Italiam contra Tiberinaque longe

          ostia, dives opum studiisque asperrima belli;

15   quam Iuno fertur terris magis omnibus unam

          posthabita coluisse Samo: hic illius arma,

          hic currus fuit; hoc regnum dea gentibus esse,

18   si qua fata sinant, iam tum tenditque fovetque.

          Progeniem sed enim Troiano a sanguine duci

          audierat Tyrias olim quae verteret arces;

21 *latē rēgem*: lit. "widely king." Early American claims of "manifest destiny" echoed Virgil's imperial theme, repeatedly stressed in the Aeneid. Aeneas' mission is all-important because Rome will rule--and civilize--most of the world as it was then known.

22 *Parcas*: Fate is a major force in Virgil's view of history. The Stoics, like the Christians later, believed in an overarching providence whose course was ultimately beneficial for mankind.

23 *Saturnia*: Juno, daughter of Saturn; her husband/brother Jove is Saturnius.

24 *ad Troiam*, etc.: Other motives for Juno's vendetta. She favored the Argive Greeks against the Trojans in the recent war; she was insulted years earlier when the Trojan prince Paris judged Venus more beautiful; she was affronted when another Trojan prince, Ganymede, was taken by Jove to be his cupbearer and sexual companion. Juno's portrayal as spiteful, vindictive, and unable to forget a grudge is an exaggeration of Homer's image of Hera in the Iliad.

accendo, ere, i, ensus: incense
Achillēs, is, m: Achilles
ad: to, at
aequor, oris, n: sea
altus, a, um: high, deep
animus, i, m: mind, spirit
arceo, ēre, ui: keep off or away
Argi, orum, m: Argives; the Greeks
atque: and, also
bellum, i, n: war
carus, a, um: dear
causa, ae, f: cause
Danaus, a, um: Danaan; Greek
dolor, ōris, m: pain, grief, anger
etiam: besides, also, even
excidium, i, n: destruction
excido, ere, i: slip out, escape
forma, ae, f: beauty, shape
Ganymēdēs, is, m: Ganymede
genus, eris, n: race, kind
gero, ere, gessi, gestus: carry on
hic haec hoc: this; he, she, it
hinc: from here, hence
honor, ōris, m: honor
iacto (1): toss, buffet
immītis, e: ungentle, harsh
iniuria, ae, f: injury, insult
invideo, ēre, vīdi, vīsus: hate
īra, ae, f: ire, wrath, passion
is, ea, id: this; he, she, it
iudicium, i, n: judgement

latē: widely, far and wide
Latium, i, n: Latium, near Rome
Libya, ae, f: northern Africa
longē: far
maneo, ēre, si, sus: remain
memor, oris: mindful, unforgetful
mens, ntis, f: mind
metuo, ere, ui: fear, dread
necdum: not yet, nor yet
Parcae, arum, f: the Fates personified
Paris, idis, m: Trojan prince
populus, i, m: people, nation
primus, a, um: first
pro: for, on behalf of
quod: because
rapio, ere ui, raptus: seize, snatch
reliquiae, arum, f: remnants
repono, ere, posui, positus: store up
rēx, rēgis, m: sovereign ruler
saevus, a, um: savage, fierce, cruel
Saturnia, ae, f: Saturn's daughter
sic: thus, so, in this manner
sperno, ere, sprēvi, sprētus: spurn
super: in addition, besides
superbus, a, um: haughty, proud
tōtus, a, um: whole, all
Troia, ae, f: Troy, Priam's city
Trōs, Trōis, m: a Trojan
venio, ire, vēni, ventus: come, go
vetus, eris: old
volvo, ere, ui, volutus: revolve, turn

--that from here a people widely sovereign and proud in war
21 hinc pŏpŭlūm lātē rēgēm bēllōquĕ sŭpērbŭm

would come to the destruction of Libya: so turned the fates.
vēntūrum‿excĭdĭō Lĭbўae: sīc vōlvĕrĕ Pārcās.

Fearing this and mindful of the old war, Saturnia,
Id mĕtŭēns vĕtĕrīsquĕ mĕmōr Sātūrnĭă bēllī,

foremost because at Troy she had carried on for (her) dear Argos
24 prīmă quŏd ād Trōĭām prō cārīs gēssĕrăt Ārgīs

(besides, not yet had the causes of her rage and fierce grief
(nēcdum‿ĕtĭăm cāusae‿īrārūm sāevīquĕ dŏlōrēs

left her mind; there remains stored up in her deep mind
excĭdĕrānt ănĭmō; mănĕt āltā mēntĕ rĕpōstŭm

the judgement of Paris and the insult of her scorned beauty
27 iūdĭcĭūm Părĭdīs sprētaeque‿īnĭūrĭă fōrmae

and the hated race and the honors of kidnapped Ganymede)--
et gĕnŭs īnvīsum‿et rāptī Gănўmēdĭs hŏnōrēs)--

incensed by these besides, she was keeping the Trojans, tossed all over the sea,
hīs āccēnsă sŭpēr ĭactātōs āequŏrĕ tōtŏ

those left (alive) by the Greeks and ungentle Achilles,
30 Trōās, rēlĭqŭĭās Dănăum‿ātque‿īmmītĭs Ăchīllī,

far from Latium, ...
ārcēbāt lōngē Lătĭō,...

Zeus and Ganymede

EXERCISES

1. *Venturum [esse]* (line 20) is a future active infinitive. Review the summary of infinitive constructions on page 17, then explain the syntax of this infinitive: how does it function in the sentence which began on line 19?

2. There are seven participles in this selection. Explain what noun each Latin participle modifies and agrees with in gender, number, and case.

3. There are ten ablatives in seven ablative constructions here, including two ablatives of separation, an idiomatic ablative with a preposition, an ablative of respect (in respect to--), an ablative of means, and two locative ablatives (place where). Explain the syntax of each.

 EXAMPLE: *alta mente* (26): locative ablative, depending on *repostum* (tells where the old offenses lay stored up).

4. Virgil has exercised poetic license in the form of *manet*, which should properly be *manent*. What are its subjects?

5. Such luxuries as commas and parentheses were unknown to ancient writers. Instead, Virgil uses a conjunction and an adverb to open and close his parenthetical statement in lines 25 ff. Identify these words.

Deer hunt; mosaic signed by Gnosis, 320-300 B.C., at Pella, Greece. Note the "signature" above the hunters: ΓΝΩΣΙΣ ΕΠΟΗΣΕΝ, "Gnosis made [me]".

21   hinc populum late regem belloque superbum

venturum excidio Libyae: sic volvere Parcas.

Id metuens veterisque memor Saturnia belli,

24   prima quod ad Troiam pro caris gesserat Argis

necdum etiam causae irarum saevique dolores

exciderant animo; manet alta mente repostum

27   iudicium Paridis spretaeque iniuriae formae

et genus invisum et rapti Ganymedis honores)--

his accensa super iactatos aequore toto

30   Troas, reliquias Danaum atque immitis Achilli,

arcebat longe Latio,...

The three Parcae, or Fates.
Clotho spins the thread of life;
Lachesis determines its length,
Atropos cuts it off.

32 errabant: in Book 3 Aeneas will tell Dido about the wanderings of his people after the sack of Troy. Their search for a homeland nears its end as Aeneas nears Italy--hence Juno's determination to stop him. In traditional epic fashion, Virgil begins his story *in medias res.*

33 tantae molis: genitive of description with *condere.*

34 Siculae: see map, p. 39. Aeneas and his people have been guests of King Acestes on the NW corner of Sicily. Now they are headed toward Italy on a northeasterly course, but Juno will see to it that a storm blows them the other way, to Carthage--and Dido.

37 mene incepto desistere...nec posse: a repudiating infinitive or exclamatory question (see p. 17), this might be called a "what, me worry?" construction.

38 Teucrorum: Virgil liked to use alternate names, like Homer, who called the Greeks Danaans, Argives, or Achaeans. Thus Juno is sometimes Saturnia, the Trojans Teucri (after their founder Teucer), Italy Hesperia or Latium.

39 Quippe: sarcastic. Juno is spitting mad, and jealously compares her impotent rage to the deadly anger of *Pallas* Athene (the Roman Minerva) who wrecked much of the Greek fleet returning from Troy because Ajax had desecrated her temple during the sack of Troy.

aes, aeris, n: bronze (on ship's prow)
aeternus, a, um: eternal
ago, agere, ēgi, actus: drive
altum, i, n: the deep [sea]
annus, i, m: year
Argīvus, a, um: Argive, Greek
atque: and, also
āverto, ere, i, rsus: avert
circum: around
classis, is, f: fleet
condo, ere, didi, ditus: found, build
conspectus, ūs, m: sight, view
cum: when, with
desisto, ere, stiti, stitus: desist
do, dare, dedi, datus: set (a sail)
ē, ex: out of, from
erat: see *sum*
erro (1): stray, wander
exuro, ere ussi, ustus: burn
fātum, i, n: fate
gens, gentis, f: clan, race, nation
hic haec hoc: this
incipio, ere, cēpi, ceptus: undertake
ipse ipsa ipsum: him/her/itself
Italia, ae, f: Italy
Iuno, onis, f: Juno
laetus, a, um: happy
mare, is, n: sea
mēne: emphatic form of accus. me

mōlēs, is, f: mass, burden
multus, a, um: much, many
nec, neque: nor, neither, and not
omnis, e: all, every
Pallas, adis, f: Athena, Minerva
pectus, oris, n: breast, heart
per: through
pontus, i, m: sea
possum, posse, potui: be able
quippe: surely, indeed
rēx, rēgis, m: king
Romanus, a, um: Roman
ruo, ere, i, rutus: rush, plow up
sal, salis, n: salt; the salt sea
sēcum: se+cum: with him/her/itself
servo (1): keep, preserve
Siculus, a, um: Sicilian
spūma, ae, f: foam
sub: under, beneath
sum, esse, fui, futurus: be
summergo, ere, mersi, mersus: sink
tantus, a, um: so great
tellūs, ūris, f: land
Teucri, orum, m: Trojans, Teucrians
vēlum, i, n: cloth, canvas, sail
veto, āre, ui, itus: veto, forbid
vinco, ere, vici, victus: defeat
vix: scarcely
vulnus, eris, n: wound

and through many years
mūltōsquĕ pĕr ānnŏs

they were wandering, driven by the fates, around all the seas.
ērrābānt āctī fātīs mărĭa͜omnĭă cīrcŭm.

33 *Of so great a burden it was to found the Roman race.*
Tāntāe mōlĭs ĕrāt Rōmānām cōndĕrĕ gēntĕm.

Scarcely out of sight of the Sicilian land onto the deep
Vīx ē cōnspēctū Sĭcŭlāe tēllūrĭs ĭn āltŭm

they were setting their sails happily and plowing the foam of the salt
vēlă dăbānt lāetĭ͜et spūmās sălĭs āerĕ rŭēbānt, *(sea) with bronze (prow)*

36 *when Juno, keeping the eternal wound beneath her breast,*
cŭm Iūnō͜aetērnŭm sērvāns sŭb pēctŏrĕ vūlnŭs

(said) these things to herself: "(What,) me, defeated, desist from my
hāec sēcŭm: "Mēnĕ͜incēptō dēsīstĕrĕ vīctăm   *undertaking*

and not be able to avert the king of the Teucrians from Italy?
nēc pōssĕ͜Ĭtălĭă Tēucrōrŭm͜āvērtĕrĕ rēgĕm?

39 *Surely I am forbidden by the fates! Was Pallas able to burn the fleet*
Quīppĕ vĕtōr fātīs. Pāllāsnĕ͜exūrĕrĕ clāssĕm

of the Argives and submerge themselves in the sea
Ārgīvŭm͜ātquĕ͜ipsōs pŏtŭĭt sūmmērgĕrĕ pōntō

*Livia Drusilla, wife of the Emperor Augustus
and mother of his successor Tiberius.*

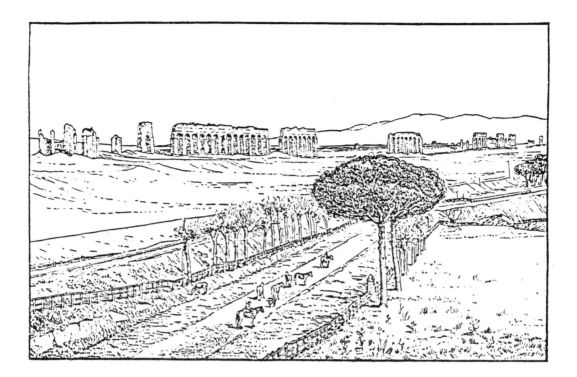

EXERCISES

N.B.: All exercises are designed to be written AFTER you have reviewed the material in each lesson. Study the Latin text, translation, notes, and vocabulary before attempting to answer any questions.

1. Explain how the term *in medias res* is used as an English expression.

2. Who were the Argives?

3. Review the syntax of the infinitive on p. 17, and explain the six infinitive constructions in this passage; all but one of them are dependent on some finite verb as subject or object. Be sure to specify which verb.

4. Identify the prepositional phrases in the Latin text.

5. Find at least eight places in this passage where the Latin has done without a preposition which an English translation must supply.

6. Find a genitive of description, and a noun which has been made up out of a verb (see page 20 bottom).

multosque per annos

errabant acti fatis maria omnia circum.

33 Tantae molis erat Romanam condere gentem.

Vix e conspectu Siculae telluris in altum

vela dabant laeti et spumas salis aere ruebant,

36 cum Iuno aeternum servans sub pectore vulnus

haec secum: "Mene incepto desistere victam

nec posse Italia Teucrorum avertere regem?

39 Quippe vetor fatis. Pallasne exurere classem

Argivum atque ipsos potuit summergere ponto

41 *noxam*: Ajax raped Cassandra in the temple of Pallas Athene at Troy while the city burned. His punishment, described here, suggests what Juno would like to do to Aeneas (who is innocent of any crime, however). This Ajax, son of Oileus, is not to be confused with the greater Ajax, son of Telamon, who also fought at Troy.

42 *ipsa*: an emphatic reference to Pallas, who wouldn't normally throw Jove's lightning.

46 *ast*: an amplified form of *at* "but," used for bitter emphasis as Juno compares her impotence to the power of a supposedly lesser deity. Juno is very rank-conscious.

48 *numen*: there is no English equivalent to this word, originally "a motion of the head, a nod" (OLD). It denotes divine power or influence, supernatural force, divine majesty, etc. The English "numen" is "a spirit believed to inhabit a natural object, phenomenon, locality" (Webster[7]).

49 *honorem*: any sacrifice, conferring status on the god to whom it is offered.

50 *flammato...corde volutans*: Virgil presents anger as one of the curses of human life. Of all uncontrolled emotions, it is anger which causes the greatest tragedies in the Aeneid, and the greatest confusion of mind. Virgil undoubtedly saw this as his "Iliadic" theme, because the thematic first word of the Iliad is "anger" and Virgil's contemporaries read the Iliad as a tragedy of anger. The Christians made anger one of the seven deadly sins.

---

acūtus, a, um: sharp
adoro (1): pray to, worship
aequor, oris, n: sea
Aiax, acis, m: Ajax, a Greek hero
annus, i, m: year
āra, ae, f: altar
ast, at: but, yet, however
aut: or
bellum, i, n: war
coniunx, iugis, m/f: spouse
cor, cordis, n: heart
corripio, ere, ui, reptus: snatch up
cum: with; when
dea, ae, f: goddess
disicio, ere, iēci, iectus: scatter
dīvus, i, m: god
e, ex: out of, from
ego: I
ēverto, ere, i, rsus: upset
exspīro (1): breathe out
flamma, ae, f: fire
flammo (1): kindle, inflame
furiae, arum, f: madness, frenzy
gens, gentis, f: clan, race, nation
gero, ere, gessi, gestus: carry on
honor, ōris, m: honor (see note)
iaculor, ari, atus: hurl, throw
ignis, is, m: fire, lightning
ille illa illud: that; he, she, it

impono, ere, posui, positus: place on
incēdo, ere, cessi, cessus: proceed
infīgo, ere, xi, xus: impale
Iovis: genitive of *Iuppiter*
ipse ipsa ipsum: him/her/itself
Iūnō, ōnis, f: Juno
noxa, ae, f: crime, fault
nūbēs, is, f: cloud
nūmen, inis, n: divinity (see note)
ob: on account of, because of
Oīleus, ei, m: father of Ajax
pectus, oris, n: breast, chest
praētereā: hereafter
qui quae quod: who, which
quisquam: anyone
rapidus, a, um: swift
ratis, is, f: ship
rēgīna, ae, f: queen
sēcum: se+cum: with him/her/itself
scopulus, i, m: crag
soror, ōris, f: sister
supplex, icis: suppliant
tālis, e: such, of such a sort
tot: so many (indeclinable)
transfīgo, ere, xi, xus: pierce
turbo, inis, m: whirlwind
ūnus, a, um: one, a single
ventus, i, m: wind
volūto: turn over, ponder

because of one man's fault and the madness of Ajax son of Oïleus?
unius ob noxam et furias Aiacis Oïlei?

She herself having thrown Jove's rapid fire from the clouds
42 Ipsa Iovis rapidum iaculata e nubibus ignem

both scattered their ships and upset the seas with winds;
disiecitque rates evertitque aequora ventis;

him (Ajax), breathing out flames from his pierced breast,
illum exspirantem transfixo pectore flammas

she snatched up with a whirlwind and impaled on a sharp crag;
45 turbine corripuit scopuloque infixit acuto;

but I, who walk proudly as queen of the gods and Jove's
ast ego, quae divum incedo regina Iovisque

both sister and wife, with a single race for so many years
et soror et coniunx, una cum gente tot annos

am waging wars. And does anyone worship Juno's power
48 bella gero. Et quisquam numen Iunonis adorat

hereafter or will a suppliant place an honor on my altars?"
praeterea aut supplex aris imponet honorem?"

Turning over such things with herself in her inflamed heart
Talia flammato secum dea corde volutans ...

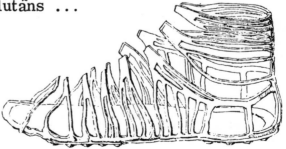

EXERCISES

N.B.: Before you begin these exercises, remember why you are reading this book in the first place. Enjoy the poetic text for its own sake; reading poetry is an end in itself, not just something you do in order to answer questions. For a suggested method of procedure, see page 38.

1. <u>Prepositions as verbal prefixes</u>: nine of the thirteen verbs in this section have prepositional prefixes which color or alter their meaning. Identify these and explain how the prefix changes each verb's meaning.

   EXAMPLE: <u>*disiecit*</u>: threw <u>apart</u>, hence "scattered"

2. There are five participles in this section. Explain the form and syntax of each, giving six or seven pieces of information for each participle.

   EXAMPLE: *iaculata*--perfect passive nominative feminine singular;
                     1   2   3   4   5

       depends on and agrees with *ipsa* (Pallas);
                            6

       takes *rapidum ignem* as its direct object.
             7

Ostia: apartments and a food shop

3. What special effects does Virgil produce by manipulating the meter of lines 44-45, making the sound imitate the sense?

unius ob noxam et furias Aiacis Oilei?

42 Ipsa Iovis rapidum iaculata e nubibus ignem

disiecitque rates evertitque aequora ventis;

illum expirantem transfixo pectore flammas

45 turbine corripuit scopuloque infixit acuto;

ast ego, quae divum incedo regina Iovisque

et soror et coniunx, una cum gente tot annos

48 bella gero. Et quisquam numen Iunonis adorat

praeterea aut supplex aris imponet honorem?"

Talia flammato secum dea corde volutans, ...

The *suovetaurilia* was a triple sacrifice of a boar (*su-*), a ram (*ove-*), and a bull (*taur-*) on the occasion of a Roman triumph.

52 *Aeoliam*: Aeolus received Odysseus briefly in Odyssey 10; here he is represented as a client deity beholden to Juno. The Romans identified Aeolia with
the windy Lipari Islands north of Sicily. See the map on p. 39.
vasto: nearly everything is large in epic; Virgil uses adjectives denoting
grandeur with great liberality.

54 *vinclis et carcere*: i.e. a restraining enclosure. Virgil expands a single
idea into two words for a grander effect. The metaphorical "chains" are in
fact a volcanic crater which incarcerates the winds. The rhetorical figure is
called "hendiadys," meaning one through two.

55 *Illi*, etc.: poets of the time were fond of painting imaginary pictures, especially of purely mythological scenes. These word-pictures are part of what
makes the Aeneid so appealing to the imagination.

56 *arce*: perhaps the highest part of the volcanic rim within which the winds
are corralled, or the core of the dead volcano.

57 *iras*: these raging winds will soon be the agents of Juno's own *ira*.

60 *pater omnipotens*: in the Aeneid Jove is more godlike than Homer's Zeus, as
Virgil's Juno is *less* godlike than her Homeric counterpart Hera. Virgil's female characters tend to be hysterical or vindictive, or both.

abdo, ere, didi, ditus: put away
ac, atque: and, also
Aeolia, ae, f: Aeolus' island
Aeolus, i, m: god of the winds
animus, i, m: mind, spirit
antrum, i, n: cavern, cave
arx, arcis, f: height, citadel
āter, tra, trum: dark, black
aura, ae, f: air
Auster, tri, m: the south wind
caelum, i, n: heaven
carcer, eris, m: prison
celsus, a, um: lofty, high
circum: around
claustrum, i, n: confining space
cum: with; when
facio, ere, fēci, factus: do, make
fero, ferre, tuli, lātus: bear, carry
fētus, a, um: teeming, pregnant
fremo, ere, ui, itus: roar
frēno (1): curb, check, restrain
furo, ere, ui: rave, rage
hīc: here
ille illa illud: that; he, she, it
imperium, i, n: command, rule
indignor, ari, atus: be indignant
īra, ae, f: anger
locus, i, m, n in plural: place
luctor, ari, atus: wrestle, struggle
magnus, a, um: large, great

mare, is, n: sea
mollio, ire, ivi, itus: mollify
mons, montis, m: mountain
murmur, uris, n: rumble, roar
ni, nisi: if not, unless
nimbus, i, m: storm cloud, cloud
omnipotens, entis: all-powerful
pater, tris, m: father
per: through
premo, ere, pressi, pressus: repress
profundus, a, um: deep, high, vast
quippe: to be sure, indeed
rapidus, a, um: swift
rēx, rēgis, m: king
sceptrum, i, n: staff of power
sēcum: sē+cum: with him/her/itself
sed: but
sedeo, ēre, sēdi, sessus: sit
sonōrus, a, um: loud-sounding
spelunca, ae, f: cave
tempero (1): control, calm
tempestas, atis, f: storm
teneo, ēre, ui, tus: hold
terra, ae, f: land
vastus, a, um: enormous
venio, ire, vēni, ventus: come, go
ventus, i, m: wind
verro, ere, i, versus: sweep, whirl
vinculum, i, n: chain, bond

into the land of the clouds, regions teeming with raging Southwinds,
51 nĭmbōrum‿ĭn pătrĭăm, lŏcă fētă fŭrēntĭbŭs Aūstrĭs,

Aeolia, she comes. Here in a vast cave king Aeolus
Aēŏlĭăm vĕnĭt. Hīc vāstō rēx Aēŏlŭs āntrŏ

controls the struggling winds and noisy tempests
lūctāntīs vēntōs tēmpēstātēsquĕ sŏnōrăs

with his rule and curbs them with bonds and an enclosure.
54 īmpĕrĭō prĕmĭt āc vīnclīs ēt cārcĕrĕ frēnăt.

They indignant, with a great rumbling of the mountain,
Īllĭ‿ĭndīgnāntēs māgnō cūm mūrmŭrĕ mōntĭs

roar about their enclosure; Aeolus sits on his lofty height
cīrcūm claūstră frĕmūnt; cēlsā sĕdĕt Aēŏlŭs ārcĕ

holding his scepter and he soothes their spirits and calms their rage;
57 scēptră tĕnēns mōllītquĕ‿ănĭmōs ēt tēmpĕrăt īrăs;

if he didn't do so, surely the rapid (winds) would bear seas and land
nī făcĭăt, mărĭă‿ac tērrās caēlūmquĕ prŏfūndŭm

and deep sky with them and sweep them through the air.
quīppĕ fĕrănt răpĭdī sēcūm vērrāntquĕ pĕr aūrăs.

But the all-powerful father (Jove) put them away in dark caves...
60 Sēd pătĕr ōmnĭpŏtēns spēlūncīs ābdĭdĭt ātrĭs ...

*Marcus Vipsanius Agrippa, who defeated
Antony and Cleopatra in the sea-battle
at Actium in 31 BC, became the Emperor's
most trusted friend and right-hand man.*

EXERCISES

1. Of the 65 words in this section, over forty have English cognates; all but five or six of these cognates are in the average college student's working vocabulary. Give an English cognate for as many of the words in this passage as possible, and confirm your theory in an English dictionary.

> EXAMPLE: *nimborum (51): nimbus*

2. In what respect is the word order in the latter part of line 52 mimetic?

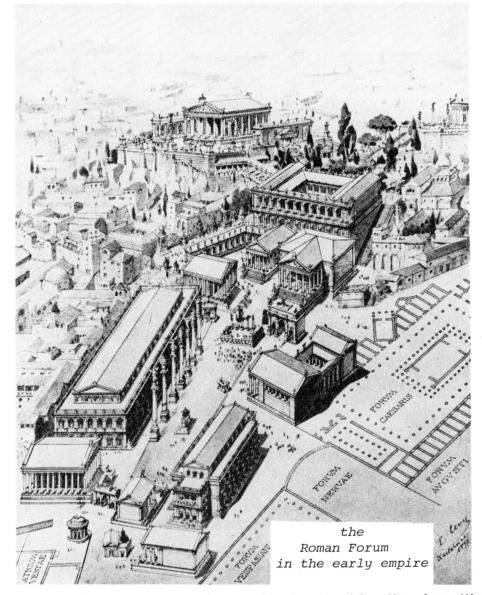

*the
Roman Forum
in the early empire*

3. Aeolus is the first authority figure in the Aeneid. How does Virgil favorably predispose us towards the exercise of authority (*imperium*) in this passage?

4. Explain the alliterative effects of lines 55-56.

51   nimborum in patriam, loca feta furentibus Austris,

Aeoliam venit. Hic vasto rex Aeolus antro

luctantis ventos tempestatesque sonoras

54   imperio premit ac vinclis et carcere frenat.

Illi indignantes magno cum murmure montis

circum claustra fremunt; celsa sedet Aeolus arce

57   sceptra tenens mollitque animos et temperat iras;

ni faciat, maria ac terras caelumque profundum

quippe ferant rapidi secum verrantque per auras.

60   Sed pater omnipotens speluncis abdidit atris ...

The Pantheon of Agrippa in Rome, ca. 118-128 A.D.

61 hoc metuens echoes 23 id metuens, where Juno fears for her native city. Jove's concern is for cosmic order--which Juno is about to upset. Zeus and Hera often worked at cross purposes in the Iliad; so here.

62 foedere is a legal term, strictly speaking "a formal agreement between states or peoples" (OLD); its use here with certo implies the care with which Jupiter has provided for the control of violent forces.

63 habenas: the latent metaphor compares the winds to half-wild horses, dangerous unless constantly held in check.

64 supplex hints at Juno's duplicity: a moment ago raging about her status, now she comes on bended knee (sub-plex = "bending under") to a minor deity.

68 Ilium...penatis: hendiadys again. Aeneas is bringing the defeated household gods of Ilium into Italy. Hendiadys allows Virgil to imply that these symbols of the city are Troy. For the ancients a city was not just an urban area but a divinely sanctioned entity. Household gods were an ancient tradition: in Genesis 31:19 Rachel steals her father's when she elopes with Jacob.

69 summersas: a proleptic adjective, the opposite of hendiadys because it compresses the idea "overwhelm and sink their ships." It anticipates the effect of obrue and speeds up the action. Juno wants swift and total destruction.

70 age diversos is proleptic again: "drive them [until they are] scattered." Juno's request leaves nothing up to Aeolus' imagination.

ad: to, towards
Aeolus, i, m: king of the winds
aequor, oris, n: the sea
ago, ere, ēgi, actus: drive
altus, a, um: high, deep
atque, ac: and, also
aut: or
certus, a, um: fixed, sure, certain
corpus, oris, n: body
disicio, ere, ieci, iectus: disperse
dīverto, ere, ti, sus: scatter
dīvus, i, m: god
do, dare, dedi, datus: give, grant
foedus, eris, n: covenant
flūctus, ūs, m: wave
gens, gentis, f: clan, nation, race
habēna, ae, f: rein
hic haec hoc: this; he, she, it
homo, hominis, m: man
Īlium, i, n: another name for Troy
impono, ere, posui, positus: impose
incutio, ere, cussi, cussus: strike
inimīcus, a, um: hostile, unfriendly
insuper: above, over
Ītalia, ae, f: also called Hesperia
iubeo, ere, iussi, iussus: order
Iūnō, ōnis, f: Juno, = Gk. Hera
laxus, a, um: loose

metuo, ere, ui: fear
mihi: dative, to me
mōles, is, f: mass, mound, heap
mōns, montis, m: mountain
mulceo, ere, lsi, lsus: calm, soothe
namque, nam: for; indeed
navigo (1): sail, navigate
obruo, ere, ui, utus: overwhelm
pater, tris, m: father
penates, ium, m: household gods
pontus, i, m: sea
porto (1): carry
premo, ere, pressi, pressus: restrain
puppis, is, f: stern; ship
qui quae quod: who, which
rēx, rēgis, m: king
scio, ire, ivi, itus: know
summergo, ere, rsi, rsus: sink
supplex, icis: like a suppliant
tibi: (dative) to you
tollo, ere, sustuli, sublatus: raise
tum: then
Tyrrhenus, a, um: Tyrrhenian, Tuscan
utor, uti, usus: (with abl.) use
ventus, i, m: wind
vinco, ere, vici, victus: conquer
vis, vis, f: force
vox, vocis, f: voice; word, speech

...fearing this, and he imposed a mass of high mountains
hōc mĕtŭēns mōlēmquĕ͡et mōntīs īnsŭpĕr āltŏs

over (them), and gave them a king who by a sure covenant
īmpŏsŭīt, rēgēmquĕ dĕdīt quī foēdĕrĕ cērtō

63 *would know both how to restrain them and how to give them loose reins*
ēt prĕmĕrĕ͡et lāxās scīrēt dărĕ iūssŭs hăbēnās.   *(when) ordered.*

To whom then Juno like a suppliant employed these words:
Ād quĕm tūm Iūnō sūpplēx hīs vōcĭbŭs ūsą͡ēst:

"Aeolus, for to you the father of gods and king of men
"Aĕŏlĕ, nāmquĕ tĭbī dīvūm pătĕr ātquĕ͡hŏmĭnūm rĕx

66 *granted both to calm the waves and raise them with wind,*
ēt mūlcērĕ dĕdīt flūctūs ēt tōllĕrĕ vēntŏ,

a race inimical to me is sailing the Tyrrhenian sea
gēns ĭnĭmīcă mĭhī Tȳrrhēnūm nāvĭgăt aēquŏr

carrying Ilium into Italy and their defeated household gods:
Īlĭum͡ĭn Ītălĭăm pōrtāns vīctōsquĕ pĕnātĭs:

69 *strike force into the winds and overwhelm their submerged ships*
īncŭtĕ vīm vēntīs sūmmērsāsquĕ͡obrŭĕ pūppĭs,

or drive them scattered and disperse their bodies on the sea.
aūt ăgĕ dīvērsōs ēt dīsĭcĕ cōrpŏră pōntŏ.

Coin of Antony and Cleopatra, whose defeat in 31 BC marked the end of organized resistance to Octavian and the beginning of the Imperial period of Roman history.

EXERCISES

1. Find:
   a. a deponent verb which takes an ablative of means instead of an accusative object;
   b. three dative constructions (see p. 6, top); one is a dative with an adjective showing relationship; the other two are indirect objects;
   c. two poetic idioms which make little sense if they are translated literally--as they are on the preceding page;
   d. six participles--identify their form and syntax, following the form suggested on page 58, #2;
   e. four imperatives.

Outdoor shrine containing household gods. Lares were tutelary gods of the hearth; Penates were gods of the larder, regarded as controlling the destiny of the household.

2. Explain the hendiadys on line 61, and give two other examples of the same rhetorical figure in lines of the Aeneid which you have already read.

3. What effect does the meter have on the quality of line 64? What does Virgil seek to accomplish thereby?

hoc metuens molemque et montis insuper altos

imposuit, regemque dedit qui foedere certo

63 et premere et laxas sciret dare iussus habenas.

Ad quem tum Iuno supplex his vocibus usa est:

"Aeole, namque tibi divum pater atque hominum rex

66 et mulcere dedit fluctus et tollere vento,

gens inimica mihi Tyrrhenum navigat aequor

Ilium in Italiam portans victosque penates:

69 incute vim ventis summersasque obrue puppis,

aut age diversos et disice corpora ponto.

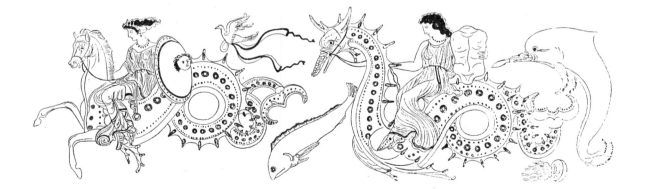

Nereids on hippocamps, bearing the armor of Achilles.

71 sunt mihi: dative of possession with a form of sum, a common idiom which gives just the right emphasis: "there are at my disposal ..."
corpore: the woman's appeal to sex is an epic theme: in Iliad 14 Hera seduces Zeus to distract him while Poseidon helps the Greeks, and she bribes the god Sleep by offering one of her Graces in marriage. In Aeneid 8 Venus makes love with Vulcan to persuade him to forge new arms for Aeneas.

73 conubio iungam: marriage among propertied families in Greece and Rome was often arranged without consulting the bride-to-be. As "first lady" in heaven, Juno is the goddess of marriage.

76 Aeolus' reply is a masterpiece of deference.

78 quodcumque hoc regni: Aeolus tactfully minimizes his importance: regni is a partitive genitive, "whatever [part] of a kingdom I have."

79 concilias defies translation, having two meanings in this context: (1) with sceptra, "procure"; with Iovem, "render favorably disposed." The English cognate "conciliate" would wrongly imply that Jove had been hostile. Aeolus is acknowledging Juno's patronage of him in the court of the gods. As her client he is obliged to do her favors. The model is the Roman patronage system.

79 accumbere: wealthy Romans dined on couches, reclining on one elbow.

accumbo, ere, cubui, cubitus: recline
Aeolus, i, m: lord of the winds
annus, i, m: year
bis: twice
capesso, ere, ivi, itus: carry out
concilio (1): win over, procure
contrā: opposite, in reply
conubium, i, m: marriage
corpus, oris, n: body
Dēiopēa, ae, f: a nymph
dico (1): dedicate, assign
dīvus, i, m: god
do, dare, dedi, datus: give
epulae, arum, f: banquet, feast
est: see *sum*
exigo, ere, ēgi, actus: pass, live out
exploro (1): examine, search out
facio, ere, fēci, factus: make
fas (indeclinable neut.): right
forma, ae, f: looks, beauty
hic haec hoc: this; he, she, it
Iovem: accus. of *Juppiter*
iungo, ere, iunxi, iunctus: join
iussum, i, n: order, command
labor, ōris, m: task
meritum, i, n: something deserved
mihi: dative, to me

nimbus, i, m: cloud
nympha, ae, f: lovely female spirit
omnis, e: all, every
opto (1): want, wish
parens, ntis, m/f: parent
potens, ntis: powerful
praesto, are, stiti, stitus: excel
prō: for, as a reward for
prōlēs, is, f: offspring
proprius, a, um: one's own
pulcher, chra, chrum: pretty
pulcherrimus, a, um: prettiest
qui quae quod: who, which
quis quid: who, what
quodcumque: whatever
rēgina, ae, f: queen
rēgnum, i, n: kingdom
sceptrum, i, n: scepter
stabilis, e: permanent, stable
sum, esse, fui, futurus: be
sunt: see *sum*
tālis, e: of such a sort
tē: accusative, you
tēcum: tē+cum: with you
tempestas, atis, f: storm
tū: nominative, you
tuus, a, um: your

I have twice seven nymphs of outstanding body
Sūnt mĭhĭ bĭs sēptēm praēstāntĭ cōrpŏrĕ nȳmphaĕ,

of whom (the one) who (is) most lovely in looks, Deiopea,
72 quārūm quaē fōrmā pūlchērrĭmă, Dēĭŏpēă,

I will join (to you) in stable wedlock and assign your own,
cōnŭbĭō iūngām stăbĭlī prŏprĭāmquĕ dĭcābŏ,

so that she may pass all the years with you for such merits
ōmnīs ūt tēcūm mĕrĭtīs prō tālĭbŭs ānnōs

and make you a parent with lovely offspring."
75 ēxĭgăt ēt pūlchrā făcĭāt tē prōlĕ părēntĕm."

Aeolus (said) these (things) in response: "(It is) your work, o queen,
Aēŏlŭs hāec cōntrā: "Tŭŭs, Ō rēgĭnă, quĭd ōptēs

to ascertain what you want; for me it is proper to carry out orders.
ēxplōrārĕ lăbōr: mĭhĭ iūssă căpēssĕrĕ fās ēst.

You procure for me whatever this (is) of a kingdom, you (procure)
78 Tū mĭhĭ quōdcūmquĕ hoc rēgnī, tū scēptră Iŏvēmquĕ

my scepter and Jove('s favor), you grant (that I) recline at the feast of
cōncĭlĭās, tū dās ĕpŭlīs āccūmbĕrĕ dīvŭm
the gods

and make (me) powerful over clouds and storms."
nīmbōrūmquĕ făcīs tēmpēstātūmquĕ pŏtēntĕm."

EXERCISES

1. Why does Aeolus repeat *tu* three times? Why does he omit the *me* as subject of *accumbere* and again as object of *facis*?

2. You have learned that ancient marriages were often arranged; what does this passage imply about marriageable girls in such situations?

3. Robert Graves' *I, Claudius* represents Augustus' wife Livia as a ruthless political intriguer who took advantage of her position as imperial consort to further her own schemes. What does this passage suggest about the system of patronage she exploited? How does the Latin expression *quid pro quo* apply to this passage?

Cameo representation of Augustus, Livia, and the boy Nero, carved in the mid-1st century A.D. when Nero's propagandists were advertising his supposed relation to the late great emperor.

--from the Hermitage collection

4. Comment on Virgil's irony in the choice of the word *meritis* in line 74: how "meritorious" is the course of action which Juno urges upon him?

5. Find: and ablative of description, a locative construction, a partitive genitive, a subject infinitive, a subjunctive clause of purpose, an object infinitive, and at least three suppressed verbs.

Sunt mihi bis septem praestanti corpore nymphae,

72 quarum quae forma pulcherrima, Deiopea,

conubio iungam stabili propriamque dicabo,

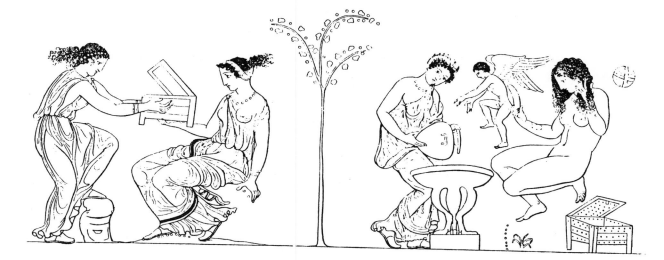

omnis ut tecum meritis pro talibus annos

75 exigat et pulchra faciat te prole parentem."

Aeolus haec contra: "Tuus, o regina, quid optes

explorare labor; mihi iussa capessere fas est.

78 Tu mihi quodcumque hoc regni, tu sceptra Iovemque

concilias, tu das epulis accumbere divum

nimborumque facis tempestatumque potentem."

81 conversa cuspide: Virgil's celebrated storm description begins as Aeolus punches a hole in the crater where the winds are corralled; they exit like water through a small irrigation dike. Virgil makes myth vivid by comparing it to everyday life, but the subtlety of his metaphor preserves epic grandeur.

84 incubuēre: alternate form of *incubuērunt;* cf. *90 intonuēre.* The switch from a historical present to the perfect tense is distracting in English, but not in Latin where the perfect can have a level of meaning called "aspect," here signaling rapid, instantaneous action. So also at 90.

85 una: adverbial--all the winds at once. This storm is a cyclone, the most terrible of storms at sea because there is no prevailing wind to run on. *Eurus, Notus, Africus:* at sea every wind has its own personality; hence the names. The worst is the gusty Africus, which blows up from Africa in the southwest. Cf. the modern sirocco, a parching, dusty wind which blows off the Sahara into Italy and Sicily.

87 virum is abbreviated from *virorum* for symmetry with *rudentum.*
strīdor is mimetic, imitating the noise of wind in the rigging.

90 intonuēre: perfect of instantaneous action (see note on 84). Virgil emphasizes the sudden violence of the storm's attack by pushing verbs to the front of lines 84, 87, 88, and 90.

a, ab: from
ac, atque: and
ad: to
aether, eris, m: upper air, sky
Africus, i, m: the southwest wind
agmen, inis, n: stream, line, course
caelum, i, n: sky
cavus, a, um: hollow
clamor, ōris, m: shouting
converto, ere, ti, rsus: turn around
crēber, bra, brum: frequent
cuspis, idis, f: spear, point
datus: see *do*
dīco, ere, dixi, dictus: say
diēs, diēi, m: day
do, dare, dedi, datus: give
ēripio, ere, ui, reptus: tear away
Eurus, i, m: the east wind
ex, ē: from, out of
facio, ere, fēci, factus: make
flūctus, ūs, m: wave
hic haec hoc: this; he/she/it
ignis, is, m: fire
impello, ere, puli, pulsus: strike
īmus, a, um: lowest, deepest
incubo, are, ui, itus: fall upon
incumbo, ere, cubui, cubitus: =incubo
insequor, i, secutus: follow
intono, are, ui: thunder, roar
latus, eris, n: side, flank

lītus, oris, n: shore
mare, is, n: sea
mico, are, ui: flash
mons, montis, m: mountain
Notus, i, m: the south wind
nox, noctis, f: night
nūbēs, is, f: cloud
oculus, i, m: eye
perflo (1): blow through
polus, i, m: pole, sky
pontus, i, m: sea
porta, ae, f: gate, opening, door
procella, ae, f: gust
quā: wherever, anywhere
rudens, entis, m: rope, line, halyard
ruo, ere, i, ruitus: rush
sēdēs, is, f: seat, base
strīdor, ōris, m: whistling, shriek
subito: suddenly
terra, ae, f: land
Teucrus, i, m: a Trojan or Teucrian
tōtus, a, um: all, whole
turbo, inis, m: whirlwind
ubi: where; when
ūnā: together, at the same time
vastus, a, um: vast
velut: as if
ventus, i, m: wind
vir, i, m: man
volvo, ere, i, volūtus: roll

When these things (were) said, with inverted spear he struck against

81 Haec ŭbĭ dīctă, căvūm cōnvērsā cūspĭdĕ mōntĕm

the hollow mountain in its side; and the winds as if having made a stream,

Īmpŭlĭt īn lătŭs; āc vēntī vĕlŭt āgmĭnĕ fāctŏ,

where an opening (is) given rush and blow through the lands in a whirl-

quā dătă pōrtă, rŭūnt ēt tērrās tūrbĭnĕ pērflānt.   *wind.*

They fell upon the sea and (through) the whole (of it) from its deepest

84 Īncŭbuĕrĕ mărī tōtūmquĕ ā sēdĭbŭs īmĭs   *beds*

together both Eurus and Notus rush and, thick with gusts,

ūnă Ēurŭsquĕ Nŏtūsquĕ rŭūnt crēbērquĕ prŏcēllĭs

Africus, and they roll vast waves to the shores.

Āfrĭcŭs ēt vāstōs vōlvūnt ād lītŏră flūctŭs:

(There) follows both the shouting of men and the screaming of ropes.

87 Īnsĕquĭtūr clāmōrquĕ vĭrūm strīdōrquĕ rŭdēntŭm.

Clouds suddenly snatch away both sky and day(light)

Ērĭpĭūnt sŭbĭtō nūbēs cāelūmquĕ dĭēmquĕ

from the eyes of the Teucrians; black night settles on the sea.

Tēucrōrum ēx ŏcŭlīs; pōntō nōx īncŭbăt ātră.

The heavens roared and the sky flashes with frequent fires ...

90 Īntŏnŭērĕ pŏlĭ ēt crēbrīs mĭcăt īgnĭbŭs āethĕr ...

CN·HELVIVM
AED·D·R·P
VESONIVS.
PRIMVS·ROG

Election notice found on a wall at Pompeii.

CN. HELVIVM AED(ilem) D(ignum) R(ei) P(ublicae) VESONIVS PRIMVS ROG(at).
(Vesonius Primus recommends you to choose as aedile Cneius Helvius, a worthy man of our city.)

EXERCISES

1. A recent commentator has remarked on the "clashing and sonorous word-music" of these lines. Explain, giving as many specifics as you can.

2. In the first exercise of Part II (p. 42) you listed all of the nominative, genitive, dative, accusative, and ablative forms separately, and explained the syntax of the ablatives. Repeat that exercise for these lines (81-90), and note any improvements in your speed and accuracy.

Eurus, the east wind

Notus, the south wind

Hellenistic Tower of the Winds in Athens,
with representations of the eight winds.

81   Haec ubi dicta, cavum conversa cuspide montem

            impulit in latus; ac venti velut agmine facto,

            qua data porta, ruunt et terras turbine perflant.

84   Incubuere mari totumque a sedibus imis

            una Eurusque Notusque ruunt creberque procellis

            Africus et vastos volvunt ad litora fluctus:

87   insequitur clamorque virum stridorque rudentum.

            Eripiunt subito nubes caelumque diemque

            Teucrorum ex oculis; ponto nox incubat atra.

90   Intonuere poli et crebris micat ignibus aether ...

Lips, the southwest wind,
corresponding to the Latin Africus

Boreas, the north wind,
corresponding to the Latin Aquilo

91: *The slow spondees and the deep n and m sounds help to make this "a magnificently sonorous line." (Williams)*

92 *Extemplo Aeneae: the first mention of Aeneas by name is preceded by a word of archaic dignity; note its slow cadence.*

93 *tendens: an operatic gesture, suitable for Aeneas' opening solo.*

94 *refert implies that Aeneas replies to the storm, though his apostrophe is to the heroes who died at Troy.*

95 *quis: abbreviated form of quibus; ante ora patrum: Virgil inserts another of his themes, the pathos of sons dying before the eyes of their fathers (who in better days would not live to see their sons die).*

97 *Tydide: Tydeus' son Diomedes wounded Aeneas in Iliad 5 and would have killed him if Aeneas' mother Aphrodite (Venus) had not rescued him.
occumbere: in a similar storm in the beginning of the Odyssey, the hero laments that he did not die at Troy. The epic hero's fear of an unheroic death goes back to the Sumerian Gilgamesh Epic where Enkidu, dying of illness, laments "happy is the man who dies in battle, for I must die in shame" (Sandars tr.). Cf. Iliad 21.279-283. Aeneas imagines himself as one of a trio of heroes dying in the defense of Troy, killed by mighty adversaries.*

(notes continued on p. 78)

Aeacidēs, ae, m: Achilles, grandson of Aeacus
Aeneas, ae, m: hero of the Aeneid
altus, a, um: high
anima, ae, f: breath, life, soul
ante: before
beātus, a, um: happy
campus, i, m: field, plain
contingo, ere, tigi, tactus: befall
corpus, oris, n: body
corripio, ere, ui, reptus: sweep up
Danaus, i, m: a Danaan or Greek
dexter, trae, f: the right hand
duplex, icis: double
effundo, ere, fūdi, fusus: pour out
extemplō: suddenly
fortis, e: brave, strong
fortissimus, a, um: mightiest
frigus, oris, n: cold, chill
galea, ae, f: helmet
gens, gentis, f: clan, race, nation
hic haec hoc: this
Hector, oris, m: hero of Troy
iaceo, ēre, ui: lie, lie dead
Iliacus, a, um: Trojan
ingemo, ere, ui: groan
ingens, entis: huge
intento (1): threaten, aim
membrum, i, n: limb, part, member
mēne: me+ne: emphatic acc., me
moenia, ium, n: walls
mors, mortis, f: death
non: not

occumbo, ere, cubui, cubitus: fall
omnis, e: all, every
oppeto, ere, ivi, itus: perish
os, oris, n: face
palma, ae, f: palm, hand
pater, tris, m: father
possum, posse, potui: be able
praesens, entis: immediate
quater: four times
qui quae quod: who, which
refero, ferre, tuli, latus: give back
saevus, a, um: fierce, savage
Sarpēdon, onis, m: a hero at Troy
scūtum, i, n: shield
sīdus, eris, n: star
Simois, entis, m: river at Troy
solvo, ere, i, solutus: relax, loosen
sub: beneath
tālis, e: such [as the following]
tēlum, i, n: weapon
tendo, ere, tetendi, tentus: extend
ter: thrice
tot: (indeclinable) so many
Troia, ae, f: Ilium
tuus, a, um: your
Tȳdīdēs, ae, m: Diomedes, Tydeus' son
ubi: where, when
unda, ae, f: wave
vir, i, m: man
volvo, ere, i, volutus: roll
vox, vocis, f: voice

and all things threaten the men with instant death.
praēsēntēmquĕ vĭrīs īntēntănt ōmnĭă mōrtĕm.

Immediately Aeneas' limbs are softened with a chill;
Extēmplo͡Aenēae͡ sōlvūntūr frĭgŏrĕ mēmbră:

he groans and holding out both hands to the stars
93 īngĕmĭt ēt dŭplĭcīs tēndēns ād sīdĕră pālmăs

makes this response with his voice: "O thrice and four times happy,
tālĭă vōcĕ rĕfērt: "Ō tērquĕ quătērquĕ bĕātī,

(you) to whom it befell to die before your fathers' faces beneath
quīs āntĕ͡ōră pătrūm Troīae sūb moēnĭbŭs āltīs

Troy's high walls! O bravest of the race of the Greeks,
96 cōntĭgĭt ōppĕtĕre! ͡Ō Dănăūm fōrtīssĭmĕ gēntīs

Tydides! (Alas) that I was not able to fall on the Trojan fields
Tydĭdĕ! Mēnĕ͡Ilĭăcīs ōccūmbĕrĕ cāmpīs

and pour out this life by means of your right hand,
nōn pŏtŭīssĕ tŭāquĕ͡ănĭmam͡hanc ēffūndĕrĕ dēxtră,

where fierce Hector lies dead by Achilles' weapon, where huge
99 saēvŭs ŭbi͡Aeăcĭdae tēlō ĭăcĕt Hēctŏr, ŭbi͡īngĕns

Sarpedon (lies), where Simois rolls beneath its waves so many
Sārpēdōn, ŭbĭ tōt Sĭmŏīs cōrrēptă sŭb ūndīs

swept-up shields of men and helmets and brave bodies!"
scūtă vĭrūm găleāsque͡et fōrtĭă cōrpŏră vōlvĭt!"

NOTES (continued)

99: Aeacidae: Achilles' patronymic "descendent of Aeacus"; Achilles' grandfather was a son of Zeus. *Hector* was Troy's chief defender, killed by Achilles in the climactic duel of the *Iliad*.

100 Sarpedon: king of the Lycians and one of the great heroes defending Troy, killed by Achilles' henchman Patroclus in *Iliad* 16.
Simois: river which flows into the Scamander at Troy. Virgil is thinking of a line in the *Iliad* where the Simois washes away the remnants of war (19.22f). Instead, the sea is washing away his fleet.

101 scuta virum echoes the opening words of the *Aeneid*. This line is echoed in turn by 119. The *virum* here is an abbreviated form of *virorum*, like *quis* for *quibus* in line 95.

"Duplicis tendens ad sidera palmas"
Engraving from a 1764 edition of the Aeneid

praesentemque viris intentant omnia mortem.

Extemplo Aeneae solvuntur frigore membra;

93   ingemit et duplicis tendens ad sidera palmas

talia voce refert: "O terque quaterque beati,

quis ante ora patrum Troiae sub moenibus altis

96   contigit oppetere! O Danaum fortissime gentis

Tydide! Mene Iliacis occumbere campis

non potuisse tuaque animam hanc effundere dextra,

99   saevus ubi Aeacidae telo iacet Hector, ubi ingens

Sarpedon, ubi tot Simois correpta sub undis

scuta virum galeasque et fortia corpora volvit!"

EXERCISES

1. Explain the case, construction, and verbal dependence of *viris* (91).
2. In the same manner as #1 above, explain the syntax of *quis* (95).
3. Most genitives depend upon a noun; on what nouns do the seven genitives in this passage depend?
4. Explain the syntax of the four infinitives in these lines (see p. 17).
5. Comment on the rhetorical tone of Aeneas' apostrophe. How is it achieved?

102 iactanti: the dialogue with the storm continues, picking up the suggestion of line 94 refert. The dative of the participle here is hard to translate; Virgil's intention was evidently to make the wind seem to answer Aeneas.

103 ad sidera: the description is subjective, not literal.

104 franguntur: the first part of the storm description (IX, before Aeneas' apostrophe) described the onset of the storm. Now we see its destructiveness.

109 Itali...aras: the "Altars" were a rock ledge between Sicily and Africa. The parenthesis involves Virgil's Italian audience by placing the storm in familiar waters. This epic tempest was long ago, but not so far away from them. "It is as if he wishes to give his readers the pleasure of looking at a map with him and of identifying the very place where these mythical events occurred." (Austin)

111 miserabile visu: the verb form is a supine in u "to denote an action in reference to which the quality [of the adjective] is asserted" (Allen & Greenough). Virgil's subjective presentation often prescribes how we should feel as well as how we should see (103 ad sidera, for example).

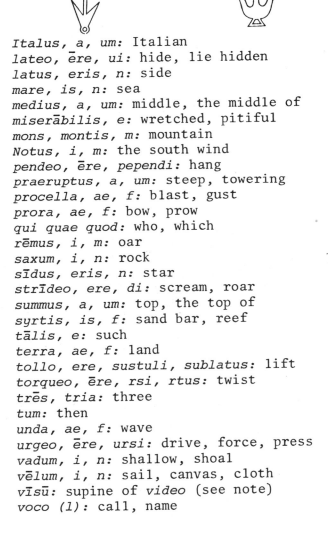

a, ab: from
abripio, ere, ui, reptus: carry off
ad: to, toward
adversus, a, um: opposite, in front
aestus, ūs, m: turbulent water
agger, eris, m: mound, bank, wall
altus, a, um: high; deep
aperio, ire, ui, ertus: open
aqua, ae, f: water
Aquilo, ōnis, m: the north wind
Arae, arum, f: the "Altars"
atque, ac: and
averto, ere, i, rsus: turn away
brevis, e: short, shallow
cingo, ere, cinxi, cinctus: encircle
cumulus, i, m: heap, mass
dehīsco, ere, hivi: gape, split, open
do, dare, dedi, datus: give, present
dorsum, i, n: back, ridge, reef
Eurus, i, m: the east wind
ferio, ire: strike, beat
fluctus, ūs, m: wave
frango, ere, frēgi, fractus: break
furo, ere, ui: rage
harēna, ae, f: sand
hic haec hoc: this
iacto (1): toss; say with emphasis
immānis, e: huge
inlīdo, ere, si, sus: dash against
insequor, i, secutus: follow, pursue
inter: between, among

Italus, a, um: Italian
lateo, ēre, ui: hide, lie hidden
latus, eris, n: side
mare, is, n: sea
medius, a, um: middle, the middle of
miserābilis, e: wretched, pitiful
mons, montis, m: mountain
Notus, i, m: the south wind
pendeo, ēre, pependi: hang
praeruptus, a, um: steep, towering
procella, ae, f: blast, gust
prora, ae, f: bow, prow
qui quae quod: who, which
rēmus, i, m: oar
saxum, i, n: rock
sīdus, eris, n: star
strīdeo, ere, di: scream, roar
summus, a, um: top, the top of
syrtis, is, f: sand bar, reef
tālis, e: such
terra, ae, f: land
tollo, ere, sustuli, sublatus: lift
torqueo, ēre, rsi, rtus: twist
trēs, tria: three
tum: then
unda, ae, f: wave
urgeo, ēre, ursi: drive, force, press
vadum, i, n: shallow, shoal
vēlum, i, n: sail, canvas, cloth
vīsū: supine of video (see note)
voco (1): call, name

To him (as he was) flinging out these words a gust roaring with the north

102 Tālĭă iāctāntī strīdēns Ăquĭlōnĕ prŏcēllă   *wind*

struck the sail head-on, and lifted the waves to the stars.

vēlum̄ādvērsă fĕrīt, flŭctūsquĕ̄ad sīdĕră tōllĭt.

Oars are broken, then the prow turns away and to the waves

Frāngūntŭr rēmī, tūm prōrą̄āvērtĭt ĕt ūndīs

presents the side; there follows in a mass a steep mountain of water.

105 dāt lătŭs; īnsĕquĭtūr cŭmŭlō praērŭptŭs ăquaē mŏns.

These hang on the top of a wave; to these a gaping wave

Hī sūmmō̄ĭn flŭctū pēndēnt; hīs ūndă dĕhīscēns

opens land between the waves; the boiling water rages with sand.

tērram̄īntēr flŭctūs ăpĕrīt; fŭrĭt aēstŭs hărēnīs.

Three (ships) Notus twists, carried off, onto hidden rocks

108 Trīs Nŏtŭs ābrēptās īn sāxă lătēntĭă tōrquĕt

(the Italians call (these) rocks which (are) in the middle of the waves

(sāxă vŏcānt Ĭtălī mĕdĭīs quaē̄ĭn flŭctĭbŭs Ārăs,   *"the Altars,"*

a great ridge on top of the sea), three Eurus forces from the deep

dōrsum̄ĭmmānĕ mărĭ sūmmō), trīs Eūrŭs ăb̄āltō

onto shallows and reefs, miserable to see,

111 īn brĕvĭą̄ēt sȳrtīs ūrgēt, mĭsĕrābĭlĕ vīsŭ,

and dashes onto shoals and encircles with a bank of sand.

īnlīdĭtquĕ vădīs ātquĕ̄āggĕrĕ cīngĭt hărēnaē.

EXERCISES

1. Virgil usually avoids one-syllable words at the end of a line. Why is the exception at the end of line 105 particularly effective?

2. In exploiting his meter for maximum effect, Virgil sometimes serves up changes of pace. Find one or two examples in these lines and explain how they enhance our impression of the storm.

3. Below are three standard translations of lines 102f. Write a paragraph about each version, explaining what it adds which was not in the original Latin, and what it omits.

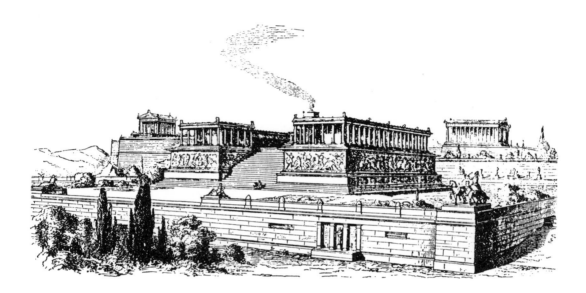

John Dryden:

> Thus while the pious prince his fate bewails,
> Fierce Boreas drove against his flying sails,
> And rent the sheets: the raging billows rise,
> And mount the tossing vessel to the skies.

Allen Mandelbaum:

> Aeneas hurled these words. The hurricane
> is howling from the north; it hammers full
> against his sails. The seas are heaved to heaven.

Robert Fitzgerald:

> As he flung out these words, a howling gust
> From due north took the sail aback and lifted
> Wavetops to heaven;

102   Talia iactanti stridens Aquilone procella

velum adversa ferit, fluctusque ad sidera tollit.

Franguntur remi, tum prora avertit et undis

105   dat latus; insequitur cumulo praeruptus aquae mons.

Hi summo in fluctu pendent; his unda dehiscens

terram inter fluctus aperit; furit aestus harenis.

108   Tris notus abreptas in saxa latentia torquet

(saxa vocant Itali mediis quae in fluctibus Aras,

dorsum immane mari summo), tris Eurus ab alto

111   in brevia et Syrtis urget, miserabile visu,

inliditque vadis atque aggere cingit harenae.

113 Oronten: Greek accusative. Of the five companions shipwrecked in this passage, only Orontes and Abas are lost forever. The others swim ashore and rejoin their countrymen. Naming these companions makes them more real to us. Aeneas later meets the ghost of Orontes at the river Styx (VI 334).

114 ipsius: used in Latin to denote the dominant personage: compare the Irish usage, e.g. "Himself just walked in."

118: "A line of great power and pity" (Austin), used more than once to describe scenes of torpedoed ships during World War II. The line--like many in Virgil--is most effective when read out loud.

120f. The metrical regularity with which these names are placed illustrates the way this storm "defeats" them, picking them off one after another.

a, ab: from
Abas, antis, m: a Trojan captain
Achatēs, ae, m: Aeneas' companion
accipio, ere, cēpi, ceptus: take in
aequor, oris, n: the sea
ago, ere, ēgi, āctus: lead, drive
Alētēs, ae, m: a Trojan leader
appāreo, ēre, ui, itus: appear
ante: before, in front of
arma, orum, n: arms
ast, at: but, yet, however
caput, itis, n: head
circum: around
compāgēs, is, f: joint, seam
excutio, ere, cussi, cussus: throw off
fatīsco, ere: split, open, gape
ferio, ire: strike
fidus, a, um: trusty, faithful
flūctus, ūs, m: wave
fortis, e: brave, strong
gaza, ae, f: treasure, wealth
grandaevus, a, um: aged, old
gurgēs, itis, m: abyss, whirlpool
hiems, emis, f: winter; storm
iam: now
ibidem: in the same place
Īlioneus, ei, m: Trojan leader
ille illa illud: that; he, she, it
imber, bris, m: rain, flood, water
ingens, entis: huge
inimīcus, a, um: unfriendly
ipse ipsa ipsum: him- her- itself

latus, eris, n: side
laxus, a, um: loose
Lycius, i, m: a male Lycian
magister, tri, m: master
nāvis, is, f: ship
nō (1): swim, float
oculus, i, m: eye
omnis, e: all, every
Orontes, is, m: comrade of Aeneas
per: through
pontus, i, m: sea
prōnus, a, um: headlong, prone
puppis, is, f: stern; ship
qui quae quod: who, which
rapidus, a, um: swift
rārus, a, um: scattered, few(pl.)
rīma, ae, f: crack
tabula, ae, f: plank, board
ter: thrice, three times
torqueo, ēre, rsi, rtus: twist
Troius, a, um: Trojan
unda, ae, f: wave
ūnus, a, um: one
validus, a, um: strong, stout
vastus, a, um: enormous
veho, ere, vexi, vectus: carry
vertex, icis, m: whirlpool ; crest
vinco, ere, vīci, victus: vanquish
vir, i, m: man
volvo, ere, i, volūtus: roll, turn
voro (1): devour, swallow up

One, which was carrying the Lycians and faithful Orontes,
Ūnām, quae Lўciōs fīdūmque vehēbat Ŏrōntem,

before his own eyes a huge sea from a crest
114 ipsius ante oculōs ingēns ā vertice pōntŭs

strikes on the stern; (its) master is thrown off and headlong
in pūppim fĕrit: ēxcŭtitūr prōnūsquĕ măgīstĕr

rolled on his head; but the ship--thrice in the same place a wave
vōlvĭtŭr īn căpŭt; āst īllām tēr flūctŭs ĭbīdēm

twists her, driving her around, and a swift whirlpool devours her with
117 tōrquĕt ăgēns cīrcum et răpĭdūs vŏrăt aequŏrĕ vērtēx.   *water.*

A few show up swimming in the vast swirl,
Appārēnt rārī nāntēs īn gūrgĭtĕ vāstŏ,

the arms of men and planks and Trojan treasure through the waves.
ārmă vĭrūm tăbŭlaeque et Trōĭă gāză pĕr ūndăs.

Now the storm has defeated the strong ship of Ilioneus, now brave
120 Iam vălĭdam Īlĭŏnei nāvēm, Iam fōrtĭs Ăchātae,   *Achates',*

and (the one) in which Abas (was) carried, and (the one) in which ancient
ēt quā vēctŭs Ăbās, ēt quā grāndaevŭs Ăletēs,   *Aletes (was carried);*

through the loose seams of their sides they all
vīcĭt hĭēms; lāxīs lătĕrūm cōmpāgĭbŭs ōmnēs

take in a hostile flood and gape with cracks.
123 ācĭpiŭnt ĭnĭmīcum īmbrēm rīmīsquĕ fătīscŭnt.

*Roman Merchantman
200. A.D.*

EXERCISES

1. Comment on the metrical pacing and the changes of pace in lines 116-118.

2. Identify the subject (and, where relevant, the object) of *vehebat* (113), *ferit* and *excutitur* (115), *volvitur* (116), *torquet* and *vorat* (117), *apparent* (118), *vicit* (122), *accipiunt*, and *fatiscunt* (123).

3. What effect might Virgil be trying to achieve by the repetitions in lines 120f.?

Roman trireme, a warship with three banks of oars

4. In line 121, why does Virgil use *grandaevus* instead on the simpler *vetus* (old)?

5. Account for the gender, number, and case of the three relative prononuns in these lines; the gender and syntax of *illam* (116), the syntax of *unam* (113), *agens* (117), *navem* (120), *Achatae* (120), and *laterum* (122).

Unam, quae Lycios fidumque vehebat Oronten,

114 ipsius ante oculos ingens a vertice pontus

in puppim ferit: excutitur pronusque magister

volvitur in caput; ast illam ter fluctus ibidem

117 torquet agens circum et rapidus vorat aequore vertex.

Apparent rari nantes in gurgite vasto,

arma virum tabulaeque et Troia gaza per undas.

120 Iam validam Ilionei navem, iam fortis Achatae,

et qua vectus Abas, et qua grandaevus Aletes,

vicit hiems; laxis laterum compagibus omnes

123 accipiunt inimicum imbrem rimisque fatiscunt.

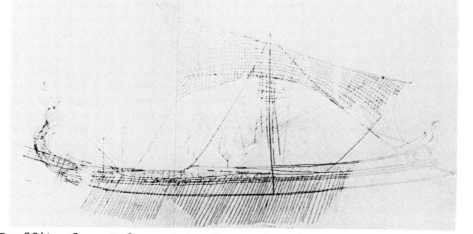

Graffito from Delos, made about the time of Virgil's birth

125 sensit governs two constructions: *(1)* the object infinitive with *misceri*, with accusative subject *pontum*; *(2)* the accusative object *hiemem*. The expression is compact in a way that English cannot be.
Neptunus: the Italian sea god, identified with the Greek Poseidon, brother of Zeus and Hades, and as such lord of the watery third of creation. His arrival brings an abrupt halt to the disorder we have been witnessing.

126 refusa: Neptune, somewhere in the depths of the sea, notices that those depths are being churned up and down; he surfaces to take a look.

129 caelique ruina: both subjective genitive (the ruin caused by the stormy sky) and objective genitive (the ruin inflicted on a previously clear sky).

130 latuēre: "escape the notice of" with accusative object *fratrem*. The idiom has no close parallel in English. Note the abbreviated form, like *tenuēre* (12). How does Neptune know what has happened? Virgil only hints. *Fratrem* implies that as Juno's brother Neptune knows from experience how she intends to misbehave. *Doli* reminds us of Juno's chronic duplicity, *irae* of her nasty temper.

131 Zephyrum: one of the gentler winds, represented in art as carrying flowers because he is a harbinger of spring.

132 generis: the winds were born of the Titan Astraeus and the dawn goddess, Eos. Neptune chides them for imagining that their divinity exempts them from punishment for disorderly conduct. He "shows the firm calmness of an autocrat who will stand no nonsense" (Austin).

ad: to
Aenēās, ae, m: Venus' son
aequor, oris, n: sea
altus, a, um: high; deep
caelum, i, n: sky; heaven
caput, itis, n: head
classis, is, f: fleet
commoveo, ēre, mōvi, mōtus: disturb
dehinc: then
disicio, ere, ieci, iectus: scatter
dolus, i, m: trickery, wiles
effero, ferre, extuli, ēlātus: lift out
ēmitto, ere, mīsi, missus: send out
Eurus, i, m: the east wind
fīdūcia, ae, f: confidence, trust
flūctus, ūs, m: wave
for fāri, fātus: say
frāter, tris, m: brother
genus, eris, n: family; descent
graviter: heavily
hiems, emis, f: storm; winter
īmus, a, um: deepest
intereā: meanwhile
īra, ae, f: anger
Iūnō, ōnis, f: Juno
lateo, ēre, ui: escape the notice of
magnus, a, um: large, great

misceo, ēre, ui, mixtus: mix up
murmur, uris, n: rumble, roar
nec, neque: nor; and not
Neptunus, i, m: lord of the sea
opprimo, ere, pressi, pressus: over-
pontus, i, m: sea   whelm
placidus, a, um: serene, calm
prospicio, ere, spexi, spectus: survey
refundo, ere, fūdi, fūsus: pour up
ruīna, ae, f: ruin
sē: accus. reflexive, him/herself
sentio, ire, sēnsi, sēnsus: perceive
stāgnum, i, n: still water
summus, a, um: top; the top of
tālis, e: such
tantus, a, um: so great
teneo, ēre, ui, tus: possess
tōtus, a, um: whole, entire
Trōs, Trōis, m: a Trojan
unda, ae, f: wave
vadum, i, n: pool
vester, tra, trum: your (pl)
video, ēre, vīdi, vīsus: see
voco (1): call
vōs: accus. pl. you
Zephyrus, i, m: the west wind

Meanwhile Neptune sensed that the sea was being mixed up with a great
Intĕrĕā māgnō mīscĕrī mūrmŭrĕ pōntŭm   *murmur*

and (he sensed) the storm sent out and from the deepest
ēmīssāmquĕ hĭĕmēm sēnsīt Nēptūnŭs ĕt īmīs

pools still waters poured up, heavily disturbed; and from the deep
126 stāgnă rĕfūsă vădīs, grăvĭtēr cōmmōtŭs; ĕt āltō

looking forth he lifted his calm head from the water's top.
prōspĭcĭēns sūmmā plăcĭdūm căpŭt ēxtŭlĭt ūndā.

He sees the fleet of Aeneas scattered over the whole sea,
Dīsīectam Aenēaē tōtō vĭdĕt aēquŏrĕ clāssēm,

the Trojans overwhelmed by the waves and by the ruin of the sky.
129 flūctĭbŭs ōpprēssōs Trōās caēlīquĕ rŭĭnă.

Nor did the tricks and anger of Juno lie hidden from her brother.
Nēc lătŭĕrĕ dŏlī frātrēm Iūnōnĭs ĕt īraē.

He calls Eurus and Zephyrus to him, then says the following:
Eurum ād sē Zĕphўrūmquĕ vŏcāt, dĕhīnc tālĭă fātŭr:

"Has so great a faith in your race possessed you?
132 "Tāntănĕ vōs gĕnĕrīs tĕnŭīt fīdūcĭă vēstrī ?...

Zephyrus, the west wind

EXERCISES

1. Comment briefly on the word music of line 124.

2. What or who is *graviter commotus* in line 126, and how do we know?

3. What is the third object of *sensit* (125)?

A Roman corbita or merchantman

4. What accusatives depend as objects on the verb *videt* (128)?

5. Explain the apparent contradiction between *graviter commotus* and *placidum caput*. What is Virgil up to this time?

6. Explain the syntax of *pontum* (124), *unda* (127), *caeli* (129), and *latuēre* (130).

Interea magno misceri murmure pontum

emissamque hiemem sensit Neptunus et imis

126   stagna refusa vadis, graviter commotus; et alto

prospiciens summa placidum caput extulit unda.

Disiectam Aeneae toto videt aequore classem,

129   fluctibus oppressos Troas caelique ruina.

Nec latuere doli fratrem Iunonis et irae.

Eurum ad se Zephyrumque vocat, dehinc talia fatur:

132   "Tantane vos generis tenuit fiducia vestri?

133 numine is close here to its radical meaning "nod," meaning divine assent.

135 quos ego--! The classic instance in our literature of aposiopesis, a fig-ure usually connected with the stage, particularly comedy. Virgil's adapta-tion is remarkable because he has transformed its effect: instead of suggest-ing an outraged person choking with impotent rage, this depicts the sensible self-control of a ruler who puts first things first: the restoration of order. Only the theatrical touch remains.

136 luetis is another idiomatic word. "Expiate" comes close to it in English: you expiate a crime with a punishment. So luetis takes the accusative com-missa as its object; non simili poenā is ablative, the means of expiation. There is to be no punishment this time, but a future offense will be another matter.

139 sorte: the story is that when they came to power the brothers Jupiter, Neptune, and Pluto chose their respective domains--earth, sea, and underworld --by lot.

140f: iactet, regnet: hortatory or jussive subjunctive, like orēmus "let us pray" and fiat lux "let there be light." See page 16, D.

143 collectasque fugit nubes: Neptune assembles the winds, then sends them home. Latin often uses a participle-verb combination where English would use two coordinate verbs: assembles and puts to flight.

Aeolus, i, m: lord of the winds
aequor, oris, n: sea
aio, ais, ait; aiunt: say
audēo, ēre, ausus sum: dare
aula, ae, f: court, hall
caelum, i, n: sky
carcer, eris, m: prison, enclosure
citius: more swiftly
claudo, ere, si, sus: close, hem in
colligo, ere, lēgi, lectus: gather
committo, ere, misi, missus: do
compono, ere, posui, positus: settle
dīco, ere dīxi, dictus: say, tell
do, dare, dedi, datus: give
domus, ūs, f: house, home
ego: I
Eurus, i, m: the east wind
flūctus, ūs, m: wave
fuga, ae, f: flight
fugo (1): put to flight
hic haec hoc: this
iacto (1): toss; vaunt; flaunt
iam: now
ille illa illud: that; he, she, it
immānis, e: immense
imperium, i, n: rule
luo, ere, i: pay or atone for
maturo (1): hasten
meus, a, um: my
mihi: (dat.) to me
misceo, ēre, ui, mixtus: stir up

mōlēs, is, f: mass, heap
moveo, ēre, mōvi, mōtus: move, etc.
non: not
nūbēs, is, f: cloud
nūmen, inis, n: divine authority
pelagus, i, n: sea
plāco (1): calm, quiet
poena, ae, f: punishment
post: afterwards; after
praesto, are, stiti, stitus: be better
qui quae quod: who; which
redūco, ere dūxi, ductus: bring back
rēgno (1): rule, reign
rēx, rēgis, m: king
saevus, a, um: fierce, savage
saxum, i, n: rock
sē: (acc.) him/her/itself
sed: but
sīc: thus, so
similis, e: similar, like
sine: without
sōl, sōlis, m: sun
sors, sortis, f: lot
tantus, a, um: so great, such
teneo, ēre, ui, tus: have, hold
terra, ae, f: earth, land
tollo, ere, sustuli, sublatus: raise
tridēns, ntis, m: 3-toothed spear
tumidus, a, um: swollen, turgid
ventus, i, m: wind
vester, tra, trum: your (pl.)

Now do you dare confuse sky and land without my divine authority, winds,
Iām caelūm tērrāmquĕ mĕō sĭnĕ nūmĭnĕ, vēntĭ,

and raise such masses (of water)?
mīscērĕ ĕt tāntās āudētĭs tōllĕrĕ mōlĕs?

(You) whom I——! But it is better to settle the raging waves.
135 Quōs ĕgŏ——! Sēd mōtōs prāestāt cōmpōnĕrĕ flūctŭs.

Afterwards you'll atone to me for things done with no similar punishment.
Pōst mĭhĭ nōn sĭmĭlī pōenā cōmmīssă lŭĕtĭs.

Hasten your flight and say these things to your king:
Mātūrātĕ fŭgām rēgīquĕ hāec dīcĭtĕ vēstrŏ:

that not to him were the command of the sea and the fierce trident
138 nōn īllī īmpĕrĭum pĕlăgī sāevūmquĕ trĭdēntĕm,

given by lot, but to me. He holds vast rocks,
sēd mĭhĭ sōrtĕ dătūm. Tĕnĕt īllĕ īmmānĭă sāxă,

your home, Eurus; in that hall let Aeolus throw himself around
vēstrās, Ēŭrĕ, dŏmōs; īllā sē īactĕt ĭn āŭlă

and rule in the closed prison of the winds."
141 Āeŏlŭs ēt clāusō vēntōrūm cārcĕrĕ rēgnĕt."

So he speaks and faster than a word he calms the swollen waters
Sīc ăĭt ēt dīctō cĭtĭŭs tŭmĭdă āequŏră plācăt

and puts to flight the gathered clouds and brings back the sun.
cōllēctāsquĕ fŭgăt nūbēs sōlēmquĕ rĕdūcĭt.

Peter Paul Rubens (1577-1640) "Quos Ego" --Neptune admonishing the winds

EXERCISES

1. The unfinished exclamation on line 135 "shows the power of an inflected language to convey meaning by case endings" (Williams). What has been left out, and how do *quos* and *ego* relate to it syntactically? Why did Neptune not finish his sentence?

2. List the twenty verb forms in this passage be mood (see lesson 4), with a separate category for participles. Explain the syntax of each participle and infinitive.

3. Identify: four direct objects; a comparative form of an adverb; three possessive adjectives; a partially suppressed infinitive; a reflexive personal pronoun.

Iam caelum terramque meo sine numine, venti,

miscere et tantas audetis tollere moles?

135   Quos ego--! Sed motos praestat componere fluctus.

Post mihi non simili poena commissa luetis.

Maturate fugam regique haec dicite vestro:

138   non illi imperium pelagi saevumque tridentem,

sed mihi sorte datum. Tenet ille immania saxa,

vestras, Eure, domos; illa se iactet in aula

141   Aeolus et clauso ventorum carcere regnet."

Sic ait et dicto citius tumida aequora placat

collectasque fugat nubes solemque reducit.

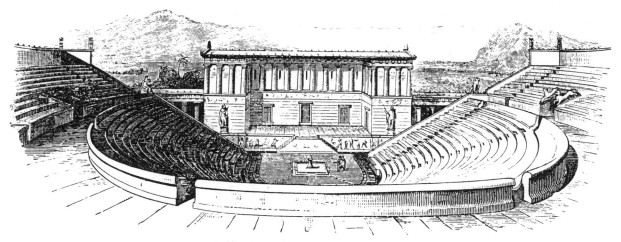

1. Theatre at Segesta. Restored by Strack.

144 Cymothöe, a Nereid or sea-nymph, aids Triton, a subsidiary sea deity, son of Neptune and Amphitrite. The description of their imagined work is pictorial in the Hellenistic tradition of post-classical Greek poetry.

148 Ac veluti: the remainder of this passage is an epic simile, prominent because it is the first in the Aeneid. This Homeric device compares an action in the story to some very different and familiar activity, as when in the Iliad Athena deflects an arrow as lightly as a mother brushing a fly from her sleeping child. Here the action brought in for comparison is a near-riot, a seditio--all too familiar to Virgil's generation, who endured constant political violence until Octavian imposed order and earned the title of Augustus, conferred by the Senate in 28 B.C. This simile is heavy with symbolic meaning as it foreshadows an epic where furor yields to order, where stormy emotions are overcome by a leader's authority and pietas.

149 ignobile has several meanings: (1) unknown, obscure; (2) low-born; and (3) inglorious, base, mean. Virgil is talking about a nasty mob: our language is less glib about the supposedly evil ways of ordinary people.

151 quem: emphatic monosyllabic line ending: any man of good reputation.

153 dictis animos: juxtaposed for emphasis on the theme: words cool off hysteria. Note how animos et pectora are bracketed by verbs of control.

ac, atque: and
acūtus, a, um: sharp
adnītor, i, xus: exert oneself
aequor, oris, n: sea
animus, i, m: spirit, mind, mood
aperio, ire, ui, ertus: open
arma, orum, n: arms
arrigo, ere, rexi, rectus: prick up
asto, are, stiti: stand near
atque, ac: and
auris, is, f: ear
conspicio, ere spexi, spectus: see
coorior, iri, ortus: arise
cum: when
Cymothöe, es, f: a Nereid, sea nymph
dētrūdo, ere, si, sus: push off
dictum, i, n: (dico) something said
fax, facis, f: torch, firebrand
forte: by chance
furor, ōris, m: frenzy, furor
gravis, e: weighty; venerable
iamque: and now
ignōbilis, e: inglorious, common
ille illa illud: that; he, she, it
ipse ipsa ipsum: he/she/itself
levis, e: light; swift
levo (1): lift, lever
magnus, a, um: large
meritum, i, n: merit; something earned
ministro (1): provide, supply
mulceo, ēre, lsi, lsus: soothe, calm
navis, is, f: ship
pectus, oris, n: breast
perlābor, i, lapsus: glide over
pietās, ātis, f: dedication to duty
populus, i, m: people, crowd
quis quid: (indefinite) some, any
rego, ere, rexi, rectus: direct
rota, ae, f: wheel
saepe: often
saevio, ire, ii, ītus: rage
saxum, i, n: rock
scopulus, i, m: lookout; cliff, crag
sēditio, ōnis, f: riot, strife
si: if
sileo, ēre, ui: become silent
simul: together
summus, a, um: top; the top of
syrtis, is, f: sand bar, reef, shoal
tempero (1): temper, calm, restrain
tridēns, entis, m: sea god's staff
Trītōn, onis, m: a minor sea deity
tum: then
unda, ae, f: wave
vastus, a, um: huge
velutī: as; just as
vir, i, m: man
volo (1): fly
vulgus, i, n: crowd; mob

Cymothoe together with Triton straining
144 Cȳmŏthŏē sĭmŭl ēt Trītōn ādnīxŭs ăcūtŏ

push off ships from a sharp rock; he himself levers with a trident
detrūdūnt nāvīs scŏpŭlō; lĕvăt ĭpsĕ trĭdēntī

and opens vast shallows and calms the sea
ēt vāstās ăpĕrīt sȳrtīs ēt tēmpĕrăt aēquŏr

and with light wheels glides over the wave tops.
147 atquĕ rŏtīs sūmmās lĕvĭbūs pērlābĭtŭr ūndās.

And just as in a great crowd when often there has arisen
Āc vĕlŭtī māgnŏ ĭn pŏpŭlō cūm saēpĕ cŏōrtă ēst

a riot and an ignoble mob rages in its mind;
sēdĭtĭō saēvītquĕ ănĭmīs īgnōbĭlĕ vūlgŭs;

and now firebrands and rocks are flying (frenzy supplies weapons),
150 iāmquĕ făcēs ēt sāxă vŏlānt, fŭrŏr ārmă mĭnīstrăt;

then if by chance they have seen some man weighty with dedication and
tūm, pĭĕtātĕ grăvem̄ ăc mĕrītīs sī fōrtĕ vĭrūm quĕm   *merits,*

they quiet down and stand near with ears pricked up;
cōnspēxērĕ, sĭlēnt ārrēctīsque aūrĭbŭs āstănt;

he directs their spirits with words and soothes their breasts:
153 īllĕ rĕgīt dīctīs ănĭmōs ēt pēctŏră mūlcēt:

Ivory tesserae,
used as theater tickets

*A founding father
as visualized by
an artist of
Virgil's time.*

*Portrait bust
identified as
that of Lucius
Junius Brutus,
founder and
first consul
of the Roman
Republic.*

EXERCISES

1. What image does Neptune acquire from the verbs of which he is the subject, as opposed to the actions of his immediate subordinates?

2. Why are the words *pietate gravem ac meritis* grouped together and pushed up to the front of the clause in which they stand?

3. Comment on the strategy of word order in line 153.

4. Identify:

    a: three deponent verbs
    b: eight direct objects
    c: thirteen conjunctions
    d: eight adverbially used ablatives or ablative phrases.

Cymothoe simul et Triton adnixus acuto

detrudunt navis scopulo; levat ipse tridenti

et vastas aperit syrtis et temperat aequor

147   atque rotis summas levibus perlabitur undas.

Ac veluti magno in populo cum saepe coorta est

seditio saevitque animis ignobile vulgus;

150   iamque faces et saxa volant, furor arma ministrat;

tum, pietate gravem ac meritis si forte virum quem

conspexere, silent arrectisque auribus astant;

153   ille regit dictis animos et pectora mulcet:

155 prospiciens: Neptune surveys his realm after calming it as he did before (*127 prospiciens*). The repetition brackets Neptune's part in the story and conveys a sense of its completion. Virgil now gives him a chariot exit in the manner of a Roman general.

157 defessi: after the serenity of a commanding Neptune, the exhaustion of the mortals.

158 Libyae: the African coast near Carthage, where the storm has driven them. *vertuntur:* passive with middle or reflexive sense: "they turn [themselves]."

159 Est...locus: like the Homeric simile in the previous section, this is a rhetorical topic, a type of description which still carries its Greek name ecphrasis (lit. "digression"), designed to establish a mood or image important for its own sake as well as for what follows. Cf. the similar formula in line 12, *urbs antiqua fuit.* This passage "forms a notable and deliberate contrast to the stress and turmoil of what has preceded" (Austin). The harbor is imaginary but lavishly described, with particular emphasis on its safety from storms.

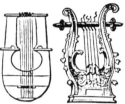

ab, a: from
ad: to
Aeneadae, arum, m: companions of Aen.
aequor, oris, n: sea; water
altum, i, n: the deep (sea)
apertus, a, um: open; clear
atque, ac: and
cado, ere, cecidi, cāsus: subside
caelum, i, n: sky, heaven
contendo, ere, i, ntus: strive
cunctus, a, um: all
currus, ūs, m: chariot
cursus, ūs, m: course
defessus, a, um: exhausted
do, dare, dedi, datus: give
efficio, ere fēci, fectus: effect
equus, i, m: horse
est (see *sum*)
flecto, ere, exi, exus: bend, steer
fragor, ōris, m: uproar, crashing
frango, ere, frēgi, fractus: break
geminus, a, um: twin
genitor, ōris, m: begetter, father
hinc: from here; on this/that side
īnsula, ae, f: island
inveho, ere, exi, ectus: carry
lātē: widely, far and wide
latus, eris, n: side
Libya, ae, f: pert of North Africa
litus, oris, n: shore
locus, i, m: place

longus, a, um: long
lōrum, i, n: rein
minor, ari, atus: threaten; tower
obiectus, ūs, m: projection, barrier
omnis, e: all; every
ōra, ae, f: shore, coast
pelagus, i, n: sea
peto, ere, ivi, itus: seek, aim at
portus, ūs, m: port, harbor, haven
postquam: after
prōspicio, ere, spexi, spectus: survey
proximus, a, um: nearest
qui quae quod: which
reductus, a, um: deep
rūpēs, is, f: crag, cliff
scindo, ere, scidi, scissus: divide
scopulus, i, m: cliff
sēcessus, ūs, m: inlet, recess
secundus, a, um: obedient; following
sēsē, sē: him/her/itself (reflexive)
sīc: so, thus
sileo, ēre, ui: be silent
sinus, ūs, m: lap; gulf, bay, inlet
sub: under
sum, esse, fui, futurus: be
tūtus, a, um: safe
unda, ae, f: wave
vastus, a, um: enormous
verto, ere, i, versus: turn
vertex, icis, m: summit, top
volo (1): fly; speed

In this way all the sea's crashing subsided, after
sīc cūnctūs pĕlăgī cĕcĭdīt frăgŏr, āequŏră pōstquăm

the father looking forth over the waters and carried through the open sky
prōspĭcĭēns gĕnĭtŏr cāelōquĕ_īnvēctŭs ăpērtŏ

turns his horses and flying along gives rein to his obedient chariot.
156 flēctĭt ĕquōs cūrrŭquĕ vŏlāns dāt lōră sĕcūndŏ.

The exhausted followers of Aeneas strive to seek in their course
Dēfēssĭ_Āenĕädāe quāe prōxĭmă lītŏră cūrsŭ

what shores (are) nearest, and turn themselves to the shores of Libya.
cōntēndūnt pĕtĕrĕ, ēt Lĭbÿāe vērtūntŭr ăd ōrăs.

There is a place in a long inlet: an island
159 Ēst īn sēcēssū lōngō lŏcŭs: īnsŭlă pōrtŭm

forms a harbor by the barrier of its sides, by which every wave from the
                                                         deep
ēffĭcĭt ōbĭēctū lătĕrŭm, quĭbŭs ōmnĭs ăb āltŏ

is broken and divides itself into deep inlets.
frăngĭtŭr īnquĕ sĭnūs scīndīt sēsĕ_ūndă rĕdūctŏs.

Here and there vast crags and twin cliffs tower menacingly
162 Hīnc ātquĕ hīnc vāstāe rūpēs gĕmĭnīquĕ mĭnāntŭr

into the sky; beneath whose tops for some distance
īn cāelŭm scŏpŭlī, quōrŭm sūb vērtĭcĕ lātĕ

safe waters lie silent;
āequŏră tūtă sĭlēnt;...

EXERCISES

1. Why are *omnis* and *unda*, which would normally go together, separared so far? Why is *reductos* taken away from *sinus*? What rhetorical term is applied to this displacement of ordinary groupings?

2. Identify: a transitive verb (explain its syntax); an intransitive verb; a deponent; a true passive; a middle; a reduplicated perfect.

3. Virgil's description of the Trojan landing place suggests safety and quiet after the storm; what romantic quality does he add to the landscape in his second sentence (162-164)? What contrasts make the scene picturesque in the manner of calendar art?

The Prima Porta statue of Augustus, probably the best known representation of Rome's first emperor, now stands in the Vatican Museum.

The Altar of Peace, begun by Augustus in 13 BC, celebrated the end of civil strife which his seizure of power eighteen years earlier had accomplished.

sic cunctus pelagi cecidit fragor, aequora postquam

prospiciens genitor caeloque invectus aperto

156   flectit equos curruque volans dat lora secundo.

Defessi Aeneadae quae proxima litora cursu

contendunt petere, et Libyae vertuntur ad oras.

159   Est in secessu longo locus: insula portum

efficit obiectu laterum, quibus omnis ab alto

frangitur inque sinus scindit sese unda reductos.

162   Hinc atque hinc vastae rupes geminique minantur

in caelum scopuli, quorum sub vertice late

aequora tuta silent;

BILL POSTED IN POMPEII.

Translation : " In the inheritance of Julia Felix, daughter of Spurius Felix, is offered to let, from the first to the sixth of the ides of August, for a term of five years, a bath called Venus's [ET NONGENIUM?], some shops, stalls, and upper rooms. They will not be let to any one exercising an infamous profession."

*164 tum an unexpected word in a static scene, but we are scanning a panorama,
now looking "backwards and upwards from the harbor" (Williams).
scaena: the scenery is nearly vertical; hence the comparison to a theater drop.
coruscis: both "shaking" in the breeze and "glittering" in the sun.*

*165 atrum nemus: dark woods, spring water, and a grotto make this scene a
classic locus amoenus ("pleasant place") like those of pastoral poetry. The
air of gentle security puts the finishing touch on Virgil's description and
emphasizes the contrast with the previous storm scene.*

*168 fessas...navis, like the tired bullocks and heifers found in loci amoeni.
non vincula: a touch of primal innocence, contributing to the golden-age mood
of pastoral. The ships float freely without harsh restraints, as if by their
own good will. Virgil wrote pastoral poetry (the Eclogues) at the beginning
of his career as a poet (45-37 B.C.).*

*174ff.: excudit...succepit...rapuit: Virgil uses forceful words to describe
the delicate work of starting a fire.*

ac, atque: and
Achātēs, ae, m: Aeneas' companion
adversus, a, um: opposite, facing
Aenēās, ae, m: our hero
alligo (1): bind, hold
amor, ōris, m: love
ancora, ae, f: anchor
antrum, i, n: cave, grotto
aqua, ae, f: water
aridus, a, um: dry
artus, ūs, m: joint; limb
atque (see ac)
āter, tra, trum: black, dark
circum: around
colligo, ere, lēgi, lectus: gather
coruscus, a, um: shaking; glittering
dēsuper: from above
do, dare, dedi, datus: give; put
domus, ūs, f: home
dulcis, e: sweet
ēgredior, i, gressus: step out
ex, ē: out, out of
excūdo, ere, di, sus: pound out
fessus, a, um: tired
flamma, ae, f: flame
folium, i, n: leaf
fōmes, itis, m: tinder
frōns, frontis: front, face, brow
harēna, ae, f: sand; beach
hīc: here
horreo, ēre, ui: bristle; tremble
hūc: to this place
ignis, is, m: fire
immineo, ēre: overhang, threaten
intus: within
lītus, oris, n: shore
magnus, a, um: large, great

morsus, ūs, m: bite
nāvis, is, f: ship
nemus, oris, n: grove, wood
non: not
numerus, i, m: number
nutrimentum, i, n: food, fuel
nympha, ae, f: a nature sprite
omnis, e: all, every
opto (1): opt, desire, wish for
pendeo, ēre, pependi: hang
pōno, ere, posui, positus: put
potior, iri, itus: take possession of
prīmum: first   (takes abl.)
rapio, ere, ui, raptus: seize
sal, salis, n: salt; salt water
saxum, i, n: rock
scaena, ae, f: theatrical backdrop
scintilla, ae, f: spark
scopulus, i, m: cliff, look-out rock
sedīle, is, n: seat
septem: seven (indeclinable)
silex, icis, m: flint
silva, ae, f: forest
sub: beneath
subeo, ire, ivi, itus: come up
succipio, ere, cēpi, ceptus: catch
tābeo, ēre: drip
tellus, ūris, f: earth, land
teneo, ēre, ui, tus: hold
Trōs, Trōis, m: a Trojan
tum: then
ullus, a, um: any
umbra, ae, f: shade
uncus, a, um: curved
vinculum, i, n: chain, bond
vīvus, a, um: alive; living

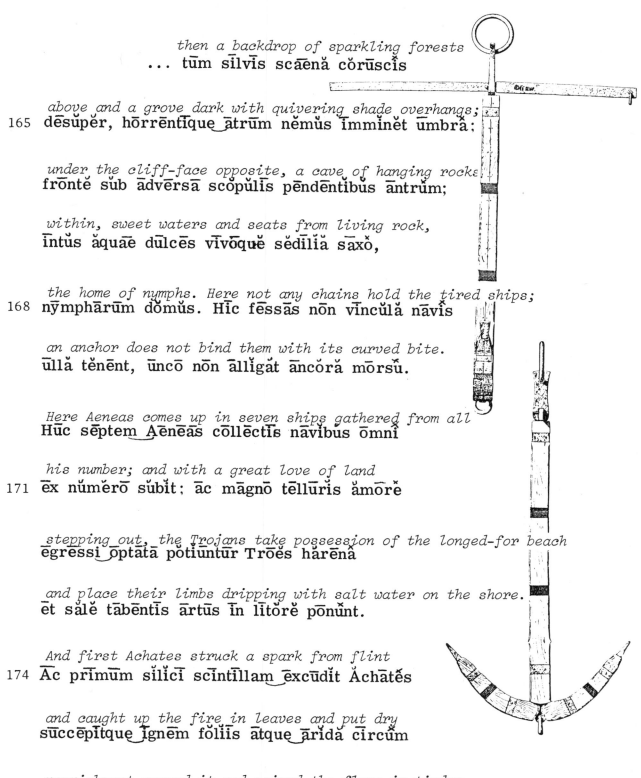

then a backdrop of sparkling forests
... tūm sĭlvīs scaēnă cŏrūscīs

above and a grove dark with quivering shade overhangs;
165 dēsŭpĕr, hōrrēntīquĕ ātrūm nĕmŭs īmmĭnĕt ūmbră;

under the cliff-face opposite, a cave of hanging rocks
frōntĕ sŭb ādvērsā scŏpŭlīs pēndēntĭbŭs āntrŭm;

within, sweet waters and seats from living rock,
īntŭs ăquaē dūlcēs vīvōquĕ sĕdīlĭă sāxŏ,

the home of nymphs. Here not any chains hold the tired ships;
168 nȳmphārūm dŏmŭs. Hīc fēssās nōn vīncŭlă nāvīs

an anchor does not bind them with its curved bite.
ūllă tĕnēnt, ūncō nōn āllĭgăt āncŏră mōrsŭ.

Here Aeneas comes up in seven ships gathered from all
Hūc sēptem Aēnēās cōllēctīs nāvĭbŭs ōmnī

his number; and with a great love of land
171 ēx nŭmĕrō sŭbĭt; āc māgnō tēllūrĭs ămōrĕ

stepping out, the Trojans take possession of the longed-for beach
ēgrēssī ōptātā pŏtiūntūr Trōĕs hărēnă

and place their limbs dripping with salt water on the shore.
ēt sălĕ tābēntīs ārtūs īn lītŏrĕ pōnŭnt.

And first Achates struck a spark from flint
174 Āc prīmūm sĭlĭcī scīntīllam ēxcūdĭt Ăchātĕs

and caught up the fire in leaves and put dry
sūccēpĭtque īgnēm fŏliīs ātque ārĭdă cīrcŭm

nourishment around it and seized the flame in tinder.
nūtrīmēntă dĕdĭt răpŭĭtque īn fōmĭtĕ flāmmăm.

Sunt lacrimae rerum: stucco head from the tomb of the Valerii, Rome.

EXERCISES

1. Virgil is sparing in his use of verbs in the first 4-5 lines of this passage. Why?

2. What elements in the continued description of the shore reinforce the impression created by *minantur* (162)? What contrasting note does Virgil then strike? Be specific.

3. Of the four primal elements (air, earth, fire, water), which ones have the Trojans just escaped, and which do they now seek out? How is this emphasized?

4. Identify: three ablatives of material
an indeclinable adjective
three fourth-declension nouns
three ablatives ending in *i*
six participles.

...tum silvis scaena coruscis

165 desuper, horrentique atrum nemus imminet umbra;

fronte sub adversa scopulis pendentibus antrum;

intus aquae dulces vivoque sedilia saxo,

168 nympharum domus. Hic fessas non vincula navis

ulla tenent, unco non alligat ancora morsu.

Huc septem Aeneas collectis navibus omni

171 ex numero subit; ac magno telluris amore

egressi optata potiuntur Troes harena

et sale tabentis artus in litore ponunt.

174 Ac primum silici scintillam excudit Achates

succepitque ignem foliis atque arida circum

nutrimenta dedit rapuitque in fomite flammam.

C·GAVIVM RVFVM II VIR
cf

VTILEM·R·P·VESONIVS·PRIMVS·ROGAT

C(aïum) GAVIVM RVFVM IIvir. O. V. F. (oro vos facite) VTILEM R(ei) P(ublicae)
VESONIVS PRIMVS ROGAT.

(Vesonius Primus recommends to your votes Caius Gavius Rufus, a man useful to your city, and
I beseech you to elect him to the office of duumvir.)

177: the rituals of fire-building and food preparation might seem trivial in epic, but they are part of the heroic routine in both the Iliad and Odyssey. *Cererem...Cerealiaque arma*: fancy epic diction for grain and cooking gear; our preference for plain diction makes such elevated language sound eccentric.

180 *scopulum*, "look-out place," is derived from the same root as our "scope."

181 *prospectum*: cf. 127, 155 *prospiciens*, also at the beginning of the line, where it was Neptune looking around (see 155 note). The echo sheds some of Neptune's majesty on Aeneas as he too reconnoiters. Appropriate words bracket the action: *scopulum* and *prospectum* at the beginning, *conspectu* and *prospicit* at the end. *Anthea* is a Greek accusative. Here Virgil names three more lost companions, all of whom later rejoin Aeneas.

182 *videat*: subjunctive with *si quem*: Aeneas doesn't actually see Antheus, but he looks around in case he *might* see "any Antheus." See page 16, B.

183 *Capyn*: another Greek accusative, a type different from *Anthea* (181).

184 *cervos*: when Odysseus lands on Circe's island in the Odyssey he goes off to reconnoiter and kills a stag for his crew. The insertion of a similar episode here invites a comparison of Libya with Circe's darkly enchanted isle.

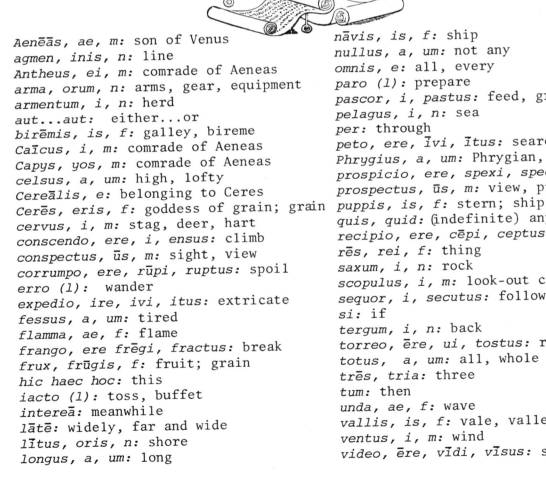

Aenēās, ae, m: son of Venus
agmen, inis, n: line
Antheus, ei, m: comrade of Aeneas
arma, orum, n: arms, gear, equipment
armentum, i, n: herd
aut...aut: either...or
birēmis, is, f: galley, bireme
Caīcus, i, m: comrade of Aeneas
Capys, yos, m: comrade of Aeneas
celsus, a, um: high, lofty
Cereālis, e: belonging to Ceres
Cerēs, eris, f: goddess of grain; grain
cervus, i, m: stag, deer, hart
conscendo, ere, i, ensus: climb
conspectus, ūs, m: sight, view
corrumpo, ere, rūpi, ruptus: spoil
erro (1): wander
expedio, ire, ivi, itus: extricate
fessus, a, um: tired
flamma, ae, f: flame
frango, ere frēgi, fractus: break
frux, frūgis, f: fruit; grain
hic haec hoc: this
iacto (1): toss, buffet
intereā: meanwhile
lātē: widely, far and wide
lītus, oris, n: shore
longus, a, um: long

nāvis, is, f: ship
nullus, a, um: not any
omnis, e: all, every
paro (1): prepare
pascor, i, pastus: feed, graze
pelagus, i, n: sea
per: through
peto, ere, īvi, ītus: search, seek
Phrygius, a, um: Phrygian, Trojan
prospicio, ere, spexi, spectus: survey
prospectus, ūs, m: view, prospect
puppis, is, f: stern; ship
quis, quid: (indefinite) any
recipio, ere, cēpi, ceptus: recover
rēs, rei, f: thing
saxum, i, n: rock
scopulus, i, m: look-out crag, cliff
sequor, i, secutus: follow
si: if
tergum, i, n: back
torreo, ēre, ui, tostus: roast
totus, a, um: all, whole
trēs, tria: three
tum: then
unda, ae, f: wave
vallis, is, f: vale, valley
ventus, i, m: wind
video, ēre, vīdi, vīsus: see

Then they bring out grain spoiled by the waves and implements of Ceres,
177 Tūm Cĕrĕrēm cōrrŭptam ūndīs Cĕrĕālĭāquĕ ārmă

tired from everything, and get ready both to roast
ēxpēdĭūnt fēssī rērūm, frūgēsquĕ rĕcēptăs

the recovered grains in flames and to crack them with stone.
ēt tōrrērĕ părānt flāmmīs ēt frāngĕrĕ sāxŏ.

Aeneas in the meantime climbs a crag, and searches
180 Aēnēās scŏpŭlum ĭntĕrĕā cōnscēndĭt, ĕt ōmnēm

the whole view far and wide on the sea, if he might see any(thing of)
prōspēctūm lātē pĕlăgō pĕtĭt, Ānthĕă sī quĕm
Antheus

thrown about by the wind, and the Phrygian biremes,
iāctātūm vēntō vĭdĕăt Phrўgĭāsquĕ bĭrēmĭs

or Capys or the arms of Caicus on his high ships.
183 aūt Căpўn aūt cēlsīs īn pūppĭbŭs ārmă Căĭcī.

He spots no ship in view, (but) three stags wandering
Nāvem īn cōnspēctū nūllām, trīs lītŏrĕ cērvŏs

on the shore; entire herds follow these
prōspĭcĭt ērrāntĭs; hōs tōtă ārmēntă sĕquūntŭr

behind, and a long line grazes through the valleys.
186 ā tērgo ēt lōngūm pēr vāllīs pāscĭtŭr āgmĕn.

EXERCISES

1. What considerations might have influenced Virgil's choice of names for the missing companions of Aeneas, judging from the construction of line 183?

2. Explain the metrical effect in line 184, and in line 186.

3. Explain the syntax of *Capyn* (183) and *errantis* (185).

Two representations of Ceres (Gk. Demeter), one a wall-painting at Pompeii, the other a statue found at Ostia.

4. What is the meaning of the suffix *-alis*?

5. What evidence could you cite from this passage to support the thesis that Virgil liked alliteration for its own sake?

177   Tum Cererem corruptam undis Cerealiaque arma

expediunt fessi rerum, frugesque receptas

et torrere parant flammis et frangere saxo.

180   Aeneas scopulum interea conscendit, et omnem

prospectum late pelago petit, Anthea si quem

iactatum vento videat Phrygiasque biremis

183   aut Capyn aut celsis in puppibus arma Caici.

Navem in conspectu nullam, tris litore cervos

prospicit errantis; hos tota armenta sequuntur

186   a tergo et longum per vallis pascitur agmen.

Kitchen utensils from Pompeii.

188 fidus...Achates: a Homeric epithet-noun combination, like "rosy-fingered dawn." This one, repeated half a dozen times in the *Aeneid*, has become an English synonym for "henchman." It was traditional for heroes to have devoted sidekicks: Achilles had Patroclus, Theseus had Pirithous. Compare today's Batman and Robin, etc.

190 cornibus arboreis: epic grandeur. Aeneas' arrows are swift (187), the stags are magnificent, their bodies gigantic (192), their antlers like trees.

192 victor: the noun is used with adverbial force, "victoriously."

194 partitur: our first example of Aeneas' *pietas*, this time to his people.

195 deinde is out of place, awkwardly interrupting a parenthesis to which it does not belong. Much of the *Aeneid* was unrevised when Virgil died in 17 BC.

196 Trinacrio: Sicilian. The island was called "Three-cornered" in Greek. See map, p. 39. *heros* is adverbial: in the manner of a Homeric ἥρως, who gave guest-gifts. This was their last stop before the storm which has just ended diverted them here to Libya.

197 pectora mulcet: like 181 *prospectum*, another echo of language and placement. It calls to mind the end of line 153.

abeo, ire, ivi, itus: go away, depart
absisto, ere, stiti: stop, desist
Acestēs, ae, m: Sicilian host of Aen.
Achates, ae, m: Aeneas' henchman
aequo (1): make equal
ago, ere ēgi, actus: drive
altus, a, um: high; deep
arboreus, a, um: tree-like
arcus, ūs, m: bow
bonus, a, um: good
cadus, i, m: jar, jug
caput, itis, n: head
celer, eris, ere: swift
consisto, ere, stiti, stitus: stop
cornū, ūs, n: horn
corpus, oris, n: body
corripio, ere, ui, reptus: snatch up
cum: with
deinde: then, next
dīco, ere, dixi, dictus: say
dīvido, ere, vīsi, vīsus: divide
do, dare, dedi, datus: give
ductor, ōris, m: leader
fero, ferre, tuli, lātus: carry
fīdus, a, um: trusty
frondeus, a, um: leafy
fundo, ere, fūdī, fūsus: lay out
gero, ere gessi, gestus: carry
hērōs, ōis, m: hero
hīc: here
hinc: from here
humus, i, f locative *humi*: ground

ingens, entis: huge
inter: among
ipse, a, um: him/her/itself
lītus, oris, n: shore
maereo, ēre: grieve
manus, ūs, f: hand
misceo, ēre, ui, mixtus: mix, confuse
mulceo, ēre, lsi, lsus: soothe, calm
navis, is, f: ship
nec, neque: nor, and...not
nemus, oris, n: grove, wood
numerus, i, m: number
omnis, e: all, every
onero (1): load
partior, iri, itus: divide, distribute
pectus, oris, n: breast, heart
peto, ere, ivi, itus: head toward
portus, ūs, m: port
primum: first
prius...quam: earlier than; before
qui quae quod: who; which
sagitta, ae, f: arrow
septem: seven (number of Aeneas' ships)
socius, i, m: comrade
sterno, ere, strāvi, strātus: lay low
tēlum, i, n: weapon
Trīnacrius, a, um: Sicilian
tum: then
turba, ae, f: crowd, herd
victor, ōris, m: victor
vīnum, i, n: wine
vulgus, i, m: crowd, throng

He stopped here and snatched up a bow in his hand and swift arrows,
Cōnstĭtĭt hīc ārcŭmquĕ mănū cĕlĕrīsquĕ săgīttăs

weapons which trusty Achates was carrying,
cōrrĭpŭīt, fīdŭs quāe tēlă gĕrēbăt Ăchātĕs,

and he lays low the leaders themselves first, carrying heads high
189 dūctōrēsque͜ īpsōs prīmūm căpĭtă͜ āltă fĕrēntĭs

with horns like trees, then the crowd and the whole mob
cōrnĭbŭs ārbŏrĕīs stērnĭt, tūm vūlgŭs ĕt ōmnĕm

he mixes up, driving them with his weapons amid the leafy groves;
mīscĕt ăgēns tēlīs nĕmŏră͜ īntēr frōndĕă tūrbăm;

nor does he stop before he victoriously lays out seven giant
192 nĕc prĭŭs ābsīstĭt quām sēptem͜ īngēntĭă vīctŏr

bodies on the ground and equals their number with the ships.
cōrpŏră fūndăt hŭmĭ͜ ēt nŭmĕrūm cūm nāvĭbŭs āequĕt.

From here he heads toward the port and distributes (them) to all his
Hīnc pōrtūm pĕtĭt ēt sŏcĭōs pārtītŭr ĭn ōmnĭs.   *companions.*

The wines which the good hero Achates had loaded in jars
195 Vīnă bŏnŭs quāe dēīndĕ cădīs ŏnĕrārăt Ăcēstĕs

on the Trinacrian shore and had given to them (as they were) departing
lītŏrĕ Trīnăcrĭō dĕdĕrātque͜ ăbĕūntĭbŭs hĕrŏs

he then divides, and soothes their grieving breasts with words:
dīvĭdĭt, ēt dīctīs māerēntĭă pēctŏră mūlcĕt:

EXERCISES

1. *Arboreis* (190) is an explicit metaphor; what latent metaphor lies half hidden in lines 189-191? What words does it depend on?

2. How do these lines affect our image of Aeneas, perhaps altering the impression we had before?

3. Give the unabbreviated form of *onerarat* (195).

4. There are five participles in these lines. Two of them are transitive and take direct objects; two are used substantively (see page 20, bottom). Identify all four and explain the syntax of each, using the format suggested on page 58, #2.

5. What other line earlier in the poem does the end of line 197 echo, and how? What words are repeated? Why would Virgil have wanted this to happen?

Wine-cart with a tank made of a bull's hide

Constitit hic arcumque manu celerisque sagittas

corripuit, fidus quae tela gerebat Achates,

189   ductoresque ipsos primum capita alta ferentis

cornibus arboreis sternit, tum vulgus et omnem

miscet agens telis nemora inter frondea turbam;

192   nec prius absistit quam septem ingentia victor

corpora fundat humi et numerum cum navibus aequet.

Hinc portum petit et socios partitur in omnis.

195   Vina bonus quae deinde cadis onerarat Acestes

litore Trinacrio dederatque abeuntibus heros

dividit, et dictis maerentia pectora mulcet:

*Aeneas' first speech echoed one of Odysseus wiching he had died a hero's death
at Troy (97 note). This is another Odyssean speech, like the one made to Odysseus' crew just before their encounter with Scylla. Aeneas' first speech was
personal; this one is public, demonstrating his self-control and leadership.*

199 deus: as often in classical poetry, this refers to no particular divinity.

201 accestis: syncopated from accessistis for euphony.

*203 forsan...iuvabit: one of the most quoted phrases in Latin. Nietzsche said
"what does not destroy me makes me strong," perhaps with this line in mind.
The memory of crises survived strengthens us for new tests. Iuvabit therefore
denotes more than just pleasure, but actual aid in time of trouble. Aeneas
has already used this argument by reminding his people of past trials survived
(o passi graviora) with the implication that they can do it again.*

*205f.: fata, fas: Aeneas retains his faith in providence and fate even though
--as we see repeatedly in the Aeneid--he is often saddened and depressed.*

*207 Durate, etc.: we now have a concise introduction to the character of Aen-
eas: passionate but self-controlled, devoted to his people and committed to
his faith that their reward awaits them in this world if they will keep their
Stoic virtues intact.*

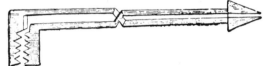

PINCERS FOR EXTRACTING FOREIGN BODIES FROM THE GULLET

accēdo, ere, cessi, cessus: approach
animus, i, m: mind, spirit, mood
ante: before the present time
cāsus, ūs, m: chance, misfortune
Cyclōpius, a, um: of the Cyclops
deus, i, m: god
discrīmen, inis, n: crisis
do, dare, dedi, datus: give
duro (1): be hard; endure
enim: for, indeed, surely
experior, iri, rtus: try, experience
fas: (indecl. n.) divine will, right
fātum, i, n: fate
finis, is, m: end
forsan: perhaps
gravior, ius: heavier; worse
hic haec hoc: this
ignārus, a, um: ignorant
illīc: there
iuvo, are, iuvi, iutus: help; please
Latium, i, n: district around Rome
maestus, a, um: sad
malum, i, n: something bad; trouble
memini, isse: remember
mitto, ere, mīsi, missus: send; dismiss
neque, nec: nor; and...not
ōlim: some time

ostendo, ere, i, ntus: offer, hold out
patior, i, passus: suffer, endure
penitus: deep
per: through
quiētus, a, um: quiet, peaceful
quoque: also
rabiēs, ēi, m: rage, fury
rēgnum, i, n: realm, rule
rēs, ei, f: thing; affair, matter
resurgo, ere, surrexi, surrectus: rise
revoco (1): recall, restore   again
saxum, i, n: rock
scopulus, i, m: cliff, crag
Scyllaeus, a, um: of Scylla
secundus, a, um: following; favorable
sēdēs, is, f: seat, habitation
servo (1): preserve
socius, i, m: comrade; ally
sono, are, ui, itus: sound, roar
tendo, ere, tetendi, tentus: strive
timor, ōris, m: fear
tot: so many
Troia, ae, f: city in Asia Minor
varius, a, um: various, different
vōs: you (nom. or acc. plural)
vōsmet: emphatic form of *vos.*

"O comrades (for neither are we before this ignorant of evils),
"Ō sŏciī (nĕquĕ ĕnim īgnārī sŭmŭs āntĕ mălōrŭm),

o you who have suffered worse things, god will grant to these also an end.
ō pāssī grăvĭōră, dăbīt dĕŭs hīs quŏquĕ fīnĕm.

You have approached Scylla's rage and the deep-sounding
Vōs ēt Scȳllāeăm răbĭēm pĕnĭtūsquĕ sŏnāntīs

crags, you have experienced also Cyclopean rocks:
201 āccēstīs scŏpŭlōs, vōs ēt Cȳclōpĭă sāxă

recall your spirits and dismiss sad fear;
ēxpērtī: rĕvŏcātĕ ănĭmōs maēstūmquĕ tĭmōrĕm

perhaps some day it will be a pleasure to remember even these things.
mīttĭtĕ: fōrsăn ĕt haēc ōlīm mĕmĭnīssĕ iŭvābĭt.

Through various misfortunes, through so many crises of things
204 Pēr vărĭōs cāsūs, pēr tōt dīscrīmĭnă rērŭm

we strive into Latium, where the fates offer
tēndĭmŭs īn Lătĭŭm, sēdēs ŭbĭ fātă quĭētās

quiet habitations; there (it is) right that the power of Troy rise again.
ōstēndūnt: īllīc fās rēgnă rĕsūrgĕrĕ Trōĭăe.

Endure, and save yourselves for favorable things."
207 Dūrātĕ, ēt vōsmēt rēbŭs sērvātĕ sĕcūndĭs. "

ROME SEATED UPON THE SEVEN HILLS.

EXERCISES

1. One commentator remarks on the "high rhetorical anaphora" in Aeneas' speech. What is he talking about?

2. Who or what was Scylla? --the Cyclops?

3. *Graviora* refers to the earlier sufferings of the Trojans such as those mentioned in lines 200-201. To what does *his quoque* (199) refer?

Rome, restored view of the temple of Mars Ultor, dedicated in 2 B.C. and part of the Forum Augusti.

4. In what sense will Aeneas' prophecy in line 206 come true? On what authority do we know it? What key words here and earlier does Virgil use to assure us of this fact?

5. Throughout the Aeneid Virgil emphasizes the note struck here by Aeneas: that the future will vindicate past and present troubles. What basic pattern of Christian belief do these lines of Virgil anticipate?

198   "O socii (neque enim ignari sumus ante malorum),

o passi graviora, dabit deus his quoque finem.

Vos et Scyllaeam rabiem penitusque sonantis

201   accestis scopulos, vos et Cyclopia saxa

experti: revocate animos maestumque timorem

mittite; forsan et haec olim meminisse iuvabit.

204   Per varios casus, per tot discrimina rerum

tendimus in Latium, sedes ubi fata quietas

ostendunt; illic fas regna resurgere Troiae.

207   Durate, et vosmet rebus servate secundis."

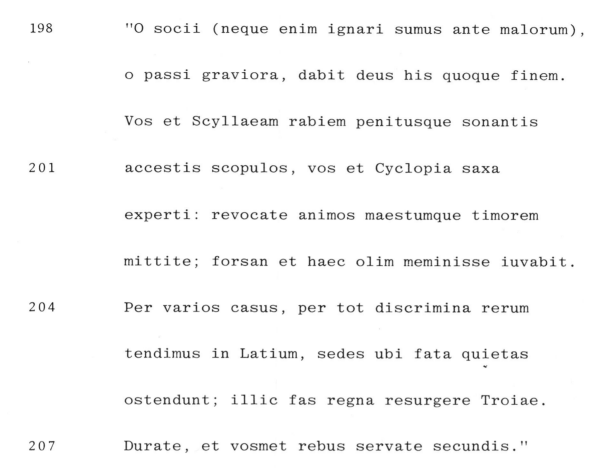

The Capitoline wolf, with Romulus and Remus

WHERE DO I GO FROM HERE?

You now should have a good sense of how Virgilian Latin works both grammatically and artistically, and why it is important to read the Aeneid in the original language. Now that you are in on the well-kept secret that it's no big deal to be a bit of a classical scholar, you may as well strike while the iron is hot. To consolidate your knowledge of mechanics, treat yourself to a thorough review of the basics to fill in the gaps left by our hasty introduction. Use Frederic M. Wheelock's *Latin: An Introductory Course Based on Ancient Authors*, published in paperback by Barnes & Noble, or Moreland & Fleischer's *Latin: An Intensive Course*, published in paperback by the University of California Press. Many colleges and universities offer courses based on these texts. An increasing number of campuses, like Northwestern, offer self-paced individualized or programmed instruction, ideal for students who are able to move ahead quickly.

An alternative to the intensive review might be to plunge directly on into the Aeneid. For that, you should try to get your hands on a copy of Clyde Pharr's *Virgil's Aeneid, Books I-VI*, published by D.C. Heath. This beautifully conceived text provides a vocabulary list and notes to accompany each page of Latin verse, with a fold-out list of the most common vocabulary in the back. It also includes a full grammatical appendix, thus providing in a single volume everything you need to go on through the first half of the Aeneid. To help you out of bad tangles and to give you a quick sense of the whole poem, you might supplement Pharr with Allen Mandelbaum's verse translation, available as a Bantam paperback, or the Fitzgerald version. The best commentary in English is that of R.D. Williams, published in two volumes with Latin text by St. Martin's Press. More detailed commentaries on individual books of the Aeneid are published by Oxford University Press. R.G. Austin prepared the commentaries on Books I, II, IV, and VI; R.D. Williams' commentaries on Books III and V belong to the same series, as does C.J. Fordyce's commentary on Books VII-VIII.

Critical books on the Aeneid are too numerous to list here; a good place to begin would be William S. Anderson's *The Art of the Aeneid* (Prentice-Hall, 1969), which includes a bibliography; or see W.A. Camps' *An Introduction To Virgil's Aeneid* (Oxford, 1969). A survey of the tradition in which Virgil wrote, with a final chapter on the Aeneid and suggestions for further reading, is Charles R. Beye's *The Iliad, the Odyssey, and the Epic Tradition* (Anchor Books, 1966).

The Sorbonne Virgil: Aeneid I, 1-30

ACKNOWLEDGEMENTS

Grateful acknowledgement is made to the following for permission to reproduce illustrations used in this book:

The Athlone Press, London, for illustration on p. 31, from Bannister Fletcher's *A History of Architecture*, © 1975 The Royal Institute of British Architects and the University of London by permission of The Athlone Press.

George Braziller, Inc., New York, for illustration on p. 106, from R.B. Bandinelli's *Rome. The Center of Power*, © 1970 George Braziller.

Deutsches Archäologisches Institut, Rome, for illustration on p. 98: photo of portrait bust in Conservatori Museum, Rome.

Hutchinson Publishing Group Limited, London, for illustration on p. 85, from William McDowell's *The Shape of Ships*, © 1952 Hutchinson.

Ionian & Popular Bank, Athens, for illustration on p. 50, deer hunt mosaic from Pella.

Mercatorfonds N.V., Antwerp, for illustration on p. 94, from J.R. Martin's *The Decorations for the Pompa Introitus Ferdinandi*, © 1972 Phaidon.

Musée de la Marine, Paris, for illustration on p. 87, photo of ship graffito from Delos.

Ny Carlsberg Glyptotek, Copenhagen, for fronticepiece/cover photo of portrait bust of Virgil, cat. no. 621.

Oxford University Press for upper map on p. 39, from Chester G. Starr's *A History of the Ancient World*, © 1965 Oxford.

Penguin Books Ltd., London, for illustrations on pp. 5, 21, 22, 23, 30, 46, 52, and 68, from A. W. Lawrence's *Greek Architecture*, © 1957, and for illustrations on pp. 58, 63, and 118, from A. Boethius & J.B. Ward-Perkins' *Etruscan and Roman Architecture*, © 1970 Penguin.

Rizzoli International Publications, Inc., New York, for illustration on p. 49, from Pierre Amiet et al., *Art In The Ancient World. A Handbook of Styles and Forms*, © 1981 Rizzoli.

Scott, Foresman and Company, Glenview, Ill., for lower map on p. 39, from Mary Johnson's *Roman Life*, © 1957 Scott, Foresman.